Transportation Center Monograph #1

LESLIE DIENES

Department of Geography

The Oder River:

Transport and Economic Development

The Oder River:
Transport and Economic Development

by
Don Edward Bierman

Published by
The Transportation Center
Northwestern University
Evanston, Illinois

Cover design by Sheila Wolfson

LESLIE DIENES
Department of Geography

To Marilyn

Table of Contents

List of Tables

List of Illustrations

Figure

Page

Introduction

The unification of geographically separated points
is the function of transportation. This view en-
ables one to consider transportation as a system of
linkages connecting different points in the spatially organized area. In this respect transportation acquires the role of an instrument by which
spatial interaction is accomplished with different
sectors of the economy and different parts of a
region. However, before the distance which separates
geographically detached places can be overcome, some
economic resources have to be expended for the
development of a circulatory system. The main objective for all carriers within this circulatory
system, both on the concentration and dispersion sides,
is to obtain maximum utility for minimum cost, thus
to provide the cheapest possible means of transporting goods and people. Nevertheless, in spite of
this common objective, each mode of transportation,
due to its inherent characteristics (in way, vehicle,
and motive power), will tend to have a competitive
advantage over other modes in moving certain types of
commodities over a certain distance.[1]
   It has been found that water carriers, in spite
of extensive terminal and transshipment costs, are
well adapted to move bulk commodities which do not
require prompt deliveries over long distances. The

[1]
 Way, vehicle, and motive power are considered here as the three major
physical components of any transportation system. For the purpose of
this book way is used interchangeably with routeway.

1

economy of water transport stems from volume operation and the relatively small range of commodities which is offered for shipment. This large quantitative and small qualitative demand imposed on water transport allows the mode to apply a greater amount of capital, in comparison with other modes, in the form of transport equipment to movement in order to obtain declining unit cost. Thus, in this case, water carriers even operating under the most adverse conditions have a substantial cost advantage over other carriers.

In addition, recently changing technology is revolutionizing the efficiency of waterborne commerce. The barge and towing vessel have introduced greater power and capacity to serve the growing number of industries that involve mass consumption of raw materials and have mass output. Therefore, industrial regions which have a significant number of steel mills, chemical, cement, papermills, petroleum refining industries, and other users of large inputs, and possessing the accessibility to a navigable body of water will find waterways an increasingly important mode of transportation.

The Oder River which has its source in Czechoslovakia, in the eastern part of the Sudeten Mountains, flows northward across present day Poland for 723 kilometers to the Baltic Sea. The navigable Oder, from the city of Koźle in Upper Silesia to the maritime port of Szczecin, a distance of 650 kilometers, flows through, in the upper reaches, and is contiguous, in the lower reaches, to the five most industrialized regions of the country.[2] This opportune location of the river gives Poland a direct water route between the concentration of heavy industry in Silesia and the maritime port of Szczecin which, in turn, makes the Oder the most important waterway in Poland.

Due to the Oder's propitious location in relation to the five industrial regions, it will play an increasingly important role in regional development by providing the means by which interregional and

[2]
Regions under investigation are Województwa Katowice, Opole, Wrocław, Zielona Góra, and Szczecin.

intraregional spatial interaction can take place. The author in this study undertakes the task of examining the function of the Oder River as an artery of transportation within the western provinces of Poland.

The organization of this volume is based on the premise that there are three logical requirements for the existing traffic on the Oder River. They are:

1) a functioning mode of transportation
2) a demanding market with terminal facilities, and
3) accessible supplies of economic goods.

On that premise, the character of the Oder waterway is analyzed. Multiple geographic techniques, including field and library research, interview, correspondence, and cartography were used.

The primary method for collecting data was field and library research. The data accumulated is presented by cartographic methods on numerous maps. This presentation provides an ideal means of locating phenomena of a particular type or showing relationships.

Identification of intervening variables was accomplished by interviews with the key officials of Zjednoczenie Żeglugi, the agency Żegluga na Odrze, Polish geographers, and a search of the literature on the topic. Much of the statistical data came from the Polish Central Statistical Office, the Polish Academy of Science, periodicals, and numerous government agencies. A study of the literature of economics, transportation, regional planning, as well as that of geography was instrumental in the application of the techniques and intellectual framework. Tables and maps are included wherever it was necessary in order to present the data which is essential to understand the study and reached conclusions.

The limitations of such a study should be noted. This study, like others dealing with Socialist countries, is also limited by the data which is available. An inventory of what can be considered strategic resources and production figures cannot be provided. Detailed breakdown of commodity shipments is not available with the degree of reliability desired. Since this is the best available information, it is currently necessary for conclusions to be reached upon the basis of this limited data. However, conditions could be changed rapidly and dramatically by new information upon the role of the Oder River on its hinterland.

This characteristic of the basic data, together with the need to make several forecasts, must be taken into account when the results of the economic analysis are considered. Although the economic analysis will present the economic position of some of the studies quantitatively, the values cannot be considered as being precise.

The study of a transportation mode and its development should begin with some knowledge of the physical environment. In Chapter II, the broad features of the environment of the Oder River basin and the characteristics of its hinterland are described. Chapter III deals with the technical aspect of the river as it may affect traffic densities. Chapter IV and V deal with the economic aspect of inland water transportation. Finally, in Chapters VI and VII, an attempt is made to analyze the role of the Oder River in the economic development within the five regions under study.

Chapter I

The Concept of Spatial Organization of Transportation and its Application to the Oder River

The role of transportation in the economic development of a region has been the subject of many studies by geographers and other scientists interested in spatial theory. For example, Ullman's studies on interaction have focused upon the importance of transportation in changing the spatial organization of man's economic endeavors.[1]

Geography is widely recognized as having important contributions to make to the study of transportation because of its concern with environmental conditions. For example, Pegrum notes that geography plays an important role in transportation as it provides the physical and natural resource base upon which traffic flows are dependent, and because physical factors exercise a great influence over transportation and traffic routes.[2] Vasilevskiy speaks of the universality of technological relationships between transportation and other branches of production which accounts for the highly "geographical"

---

[1] Edward Ullman, "The Role of Transportation and Bases of Interaction," Man's Role in Changing the Face of the Earth, ed. William L. Thomas, Jr. (Chicago: University of Chicago Press, 1956), pp. 862-880.

[2] D.F. Pegrum, Transportation: Economics and Public Policy (Homewood, Illinois: Richard D. Irwin, Inc., 1963), p. 75.

character of transportation.[3] One of these relationships can be demonstrated by the examination of
traffic flow patterns and the general location and
grouping of routes. Many of the economic limits of
transportation are established very clearly by physical conditions. These basic geographic conditions
are fundamental to the need for transportation. The
demand for transportation is rooted in stable structural forms, tied to the particular economic geography
of the country. Kansky recognized the need for study-
ing and understanding the structure of a transportation
system within the regions, hoping perhaps this would
shed light on the function of the transportation
network within the region.[4]

The planning problem facing transportation
development is the integration of the physical geography of the country with the economics of development and the economies of transportation. This need
for the integration of areas of study is a phase of
transportation planning which is essential if incor-
rect investments are to be avoided.[5] "The attributes
of alternative transport methods, then need to be
weighed in the light of the environment to be served
and the transport tasks to be performed."[6] Kaufman

3
 L.I. Vasilevskiy, "Basic Research Problems in the Geography of Trans-
portation of Capitalist and Under Developed Countries," Soviet Geography:
Review and Translation, Vol. IV, 1963, p. 36.

4
 K.J. Kansky, Structure of Transportation Networks, (Chicago: Department
of Geography Research Paper No. 84, University of Chicago, 1963).

5
 W. Owen, "Transportation and Technology," The American Economic Review,
Vol. LII, No. 2 (1962), pp. 405-414.

6
 Ibid., p. 409.

refers to geography as the "third pillar" upon which transport planning should rest.[7]

Wolfe, however, has suggested that geography should do more than contribute to the framework within which transportation operates. Geographic techniques should be able to contribute greatly to transport planning if geography is, in fact, so important in explaining transportation requirements.[8] For example, through changing the relative location of places, transportation affects the distribution of productive capacities and, thereby, the distribution of land or area values.

The integrative nature of geography and the concern for spatial interaction are both qualities needed in transportation planning. Traffic flow is dependent upon a wide variety of factors which play a part in theories of spatial interaction. In order to establish the connections between areas and the nature of the spatial interchange, it is necessary to find some way of measuring and mapping the flow of traffic, including its volume and speed of movement and its origin and destination.[9] Geographic techniques and concepts put an emphasis upon environmental and spatial concepts which have been all too absent in transportation economics.

Statement of the Problem

As a result of the Potsdam Agreement and the subsequent shift of political boundaries by approximately

[7]
J.H. Kaufman, "Planning for Transport Investment in the Development of Iran," The American Economic Review, Vol. LII, No. 2 (1962), pp. 396-404.

[8]
Roy I. Wolfe, "Contribution from Geography to Urban Transportation Research," Highway Research Board, Bulletin 326 (Washington, D.C.: National Research Council, 1962), pp. 46-48.

[9]
Preston E. James and Clarence F. Jones (eds.), American Geography: Inventory and Prospect (Syracuse: Syracuse University Press, 1954), p. 316.

135 kilometers to the west in the Post-World War II
period, Poland inherited the Oder River and its tributary the Nysa Łużycka which functions as a political boundary. The importance of the Oder, however,
stems from the fact that this sizable stream connects
the maritime port of Szczecin. In this respect it
became an important artery of transportation.

There are great benefits to the national economy
which stem from the inherent advantages that grow out
of the technical aspects of river movement. Consequently, attention is given to the significance of
these advantages, not only for the general economy
but more specifically to the region contiguous to the
Oder River. A review of the extensive literature on
the subject suggests that, in recent years, barge
transportation has become a very low cost movement
and that the service has materially improved during
the past two decades. The advantage of barge transportation stems from its inherent characteristics in
its motive power, vehicle, and way. Technological
improvements in these three components of a transport
system brought the mode, once again, into competition
with other modes. However, due to the mode's particular idiosyncrasies in motive power, vehicle, and way,
the primary requisite for utilizing the efficiencies
of barge shipment is the concentration of a massive
volume of freight at one point. This may be seen as
a shortcoming to some extent. It means that many
products and movement on the distribution side, where
break bulk of commodity occurs and where size of
shipments are relatively small, are not best suited
for barge shipments or are not likely to be shipped
by inland waterways. To exemplify these two sides
of each movement and the inherent advantage and disadvantage of the mode, it can be observed that in
the United States barge lines have minimum tenders
of 500 to 1,000 tons, where railroad carriers have
carload rates for a minimum of 12 to 15 tons. As
it appears, the requirement of such large minimum
tenders certainly restricts inland waterways as a
mode of transportation to a fairly limited range of
commodities and the type of movement.

In the past, the economic requirements of inland waterways for massive shipments has led some transport economists to the conclusion that the service is useful for only a limited portion of movement requirements. In recent years, development in the transportation sector of the economy in the United States and abroad suggests modification of this earlier reached conclusion. First, it must be pointed out that this is an era of specialized transportation. As the economic system becomes more sophisticated and as spatial interaction increases, both quantitative and qualitative demands for transportation rises. Hence, it can be said that the transportation system is highly tailored to the needs and requirements of the economy. The very fact that each mode can perform some functions very well and other functions only moderately well does not suggest that any single mode is unimportant or inferior. The trend toward specialization of carriers has continued to the present and there is every reason to expect that the trend will continue in the future. Any carrier that fails to measure up to the demand imposed on it by the economic system or attempts to be competitive in all markets may well be doomed to the point of extinction.

The second factor, which negates the common conclusion reached by some transport economists that the inland waterways are only suitable for a few localized movements, is the make-up of the United States and Polish freight traffic. It is interesting to note that in both countries, in spite of great economic differences, products of mines, which are virtually all bulk materials, measured in terms of weight constitute slightly more than 42 percent of all railroad tonnage moved.[10] Agricultural products are also

10
   U.S. Department of Commerce, Bureau of the Census, Statistical Abstract of the United States 1969 (Washington, D.C.: U.S. Government Printing Office, 1969), Table 845, p. 562.

   Główny Urząd Statystyczny, Rocznik Statystyczny 1968 (Warsaw: 1969), Table 7, p. 299.

significant and probably 50 percent or more of these are grain which is moved in bulk. The same applies to forest products. The addition of truck and inland waterway tonnage to these figures would not greatly change the relative relationships of the various commodities. Motor transport would primarily increase the manufactured goods and the barge lines would increase the bulky categories. Therefore, one can conclude that well over 40 percent of the goods, measured by weight, moved in the United States and Poland are of a low value, bulk commodity of unprocessed nature. Inland waterways, as was pointed out earlier, due to their inherent characteristics are unquestionably well suited for the inexpensive movement of bulk commodity, requiring large volumes, over long distances from the point of origin to the points of processing.

Inland water transportation routes are restricted to the navigable rivers. The lack of a complete network of routes and the lack of connectivity between various river basins is a substantial limitation to the utility of the mode. But, above all, what is extremely important is the conformity of the routes to the desired direction of movement.

In here, the assumption is made that the transportation network, whether this is a railroad network or inland waterway, performs a specific function within the region. The structure of the transportation network, defined by Kansky as a set of geographic locations interconnected in a system by a number of routes, will largely depend on the function that the system of transportation is asked to play by the economy.[11] Therefore, as the requirements or the condition within the region has changed, the structure must also change in order to fulfill its newly assigned task. Even the most casual observer of the Polish economy must admit that the economy and the economic regions are undergoing drastic change in recent years, necessitating changes in the function

[11]
Kansky, p. 1.

10

and the structure of the transportation network. The purpose of this study is to examine such a change both in structure and the function of the Oder River within five contiguous regions.

The lack of continuous statistical data for the period of several decades eliminates the possibility in using a mathematical model. This, however, should not be treated as a deterrent as one can with an equal degree of success examine the function and the structure of the Oder waterway in the framework of an intellectual model.

A model, for the purpose of this study, may be defined as a master plan, a design, or some sort of a structure intended to serve as a pattern for a thing to be made. It may also be defined as a simplified abstract representation of some complex real phenomenon in existence. It is interesting to note that Deutsch's philosophical ideas of a model are in agreement with chorological study so familiar to a geographer. Hence, Deutsch questions one's ability to completely understand total space, he sees that within a given structure any defined space can be studied and understood.[12]

The intellectual model has the value of aiding the researcher in focusing his attention on the relevant phenomena to the study in the mass totality of phenomena. It provides a functional mechanism by which data might be organized, processed, and interpreted, giving a clear picture of the nature and scope of physical and cultural phenomena.

---

[12]
Karl Deutsch, "On Communications Models in the Social Sciences," Public Opinion Quarterly, Vol. XVI (Fall, 1952), pp. 356-357.

Chapter II
The Geographic Setting

The character of the transportation activities ob-
servable in any existing economy is a reflection of
the geographic setting of that economy and a tangible
legacy of the historical interaction between the
natural environment and society. These are the forces
one discovers when seeking to determine not merely
what an economy's transportation system is like, but
why it has assumed the configuration that it has.
When questions are raised concerning the possible or
probable role of the Oder River as an artery of transportation and its influence on the industrial development, it will inevitably be found that the analysis
soon returns to consideration of the geographic setting of the river within the economy and its historical
development as the fundamental elements of the
situation.

Therefore, in the following pages it will be
advantageous to analyze first the physical characteristics of the Oder River and its drainage system.
Secondly, the hinterland of the Oder River and the
general economic condition of the area, during the
Pre-World War II period and the Post-World War II
period, is discussed under the heading of characteristics of the Oder River.

Location of the Oder River

The Oder River has its source in Czechoslovakia in
the eastern part of the Sudeten Mountains, flows
across the province of Moravia for 125 kilometers,
entering Poland through the broad tectonically produced Moravian Gate. Crossing the Polish-
Czechoslovakian boundary, the Oder rapidly changes

its course of flow, from a north-easterly to a north-westerly direction, and for approximately fifteen kilometers becomes an administrative boundary in the extreme south between the województwa of Opole and Katowice.[1]

As Figure 2.1 shows, the general direction of flow of the river in the upper and middle reaches is northwesterly across the three western województwa, Opole, Wrocław, and part of Zielona Góra, for approximately 360 kilometers to the boundary line between Poland and East Germany, where the Oder meets its major tributary, the Nysa-Łużycka, flowing from the south. At that point, once again the Oder changes its course from northwesterly to northerly and flowing northward contiguous to the northerns parts of województwa Zielona Góra and Szczecin assumes the function, in its upper reaches from the Nysa-Łużycka, as the western boundary of Poland. Above the city of Gryfino, in the województwo of Szczecin, the international boundary does not follow the confluence of the river but instead circumvents the port of Szczecin by seven kilometers to the west. This gives Poland exclusive control of the maritime port and the mouth of the river and control over the major part of the Bay of Szczecin through which the Oder discharges its waters into the Baltic Sea.

The Oder is navigable from the city of Koźle, in województwo Opole in Upper Silesia, to the maritime port of Szczecin, a distance of nearly 650 kilometers. Within this sector, only under the most ideal navigable conditions, barges not exceeding 600 tons may operate freely. Barges of markedly lesser tonnage may continue across the Czechoslovakian border of Ostrava, although very little traffic moves above the

---

[1] Województwo (singular) and województwa (plural), administrative regions of Poland, correspond to provinces of which there are seventeen in Post-World War II Poland. The name of the województwo derives from the major city in the region which is also the administrative capital of the province.

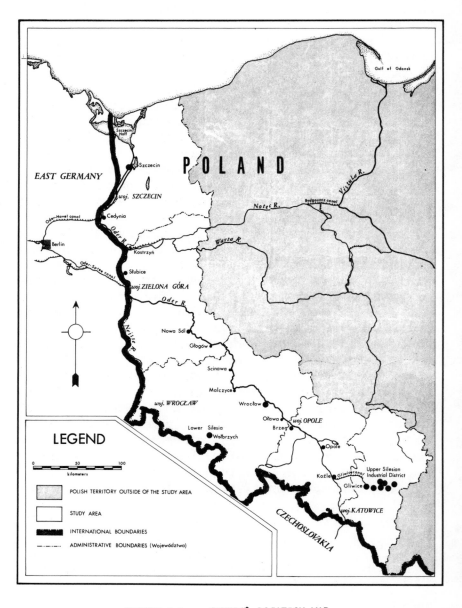

FIGURE 2.1.: GENERAL LOCATION MAP

14

confluence of the Gliwice Canal at Koźle. Figure 1.
illustrates the Oder's extremely advantageous geographic position in relation to the territory through
which it flows. It can be seen that the river above
the city of Koźle is linked by the Gliwice Canal with
the industrial region of Upper Silesia, the heart of
Poland's heavy industry. In its northwesterly flow
to the East German-Polish border, the Oder in its
upper and middle reaches traverses the industrial
regions of Upper Silesia, Lower Silesia and numerous
small industrial agglomerations which were attracted
to the river location of the województwa of Opole,
Wrocław, and Zielona Góra. On reaching the border,
with the change in direction to a northerly flow,
the Oder in its upper reaches is only contiguous to the
western side of the wojewodztwa of the northern portion
of Zielona Góra and Szczecin.

A closer look at the Oder's directional flow
shows that in spite of its general northwesterly and
northerly flow the river is in the habit of rapidly
changing its course. A full explanation for the reason of this phenomenon is beyond the scope of this
study, however, a partial explanation suggests that
structural control in the area of tectonic and glacial
origin causes the stream to rapidly change its course.
Nevertheless, the Oder laboriously progresses northward in the direction of the general slope across the
landscape of Poland until it reaches its final destination, through its incipient delta, the Baltic Sea.

Both Figure 2.2. and Table 2.1. show that almost
the entire country (99.7 percent) drains to the
Baltic basin and less than 0.3 percent to the Black
and North Sea drainage basins.

The two largest river basins in Poland, part of
the Baltic system, are the Vistula and the Oder. The
western part of the country is drained toward the
north by the Oder and its major tributary the Warta-
Noteć, while the eastern regions are drained by the
Vistula and its tributaries, the Pilica, Narew, Bug,
and Wieprz. The water divides between these two
major basins are distinct and there is virtually no
major area in Poland of indefinite drainage.

15

TABLE 2.1.

POLAND'S DRAINAGE SYSTEM

	In Square Kilometers	Percent of Total Territory
Total Polish Territory	312,677	100.0
Vistula River Basin	173,900	55.6
Oder River Basin	106,177	34.0
Other Basins Draining to the Baltic Sea	30,900	9.9
Basins Draining to the Black and North Seas	800	0.3

Source: Główny Urząd Statystyczny, Rocznik Statystyczny 1968 (Warsaw: 1969), Table 7, p. 3.

The Physical Characteristics of the Oder River Drainage System

The entire Oder River drainage basin covers 119,052 square kilometers of which 106,077 square kilometers or 89.1 percent are located in Poland.[2] The basin can be characterized as a typical one, carved by a river and its tributaries flowing on the Great European Plain, with a somewhat heterogeneous and complicated course.

As Figure 2.3. shows, the area occupied by the Oder River Basin can be divided morphologically into two major sections, the southern section, a relatively small mountainous part, and the northern section, predominantly a plain. In the southern section the Oder rises in the Oder Mountains, which are a part of the most easterly extension of the Sudeten Range, at an elevation of 634 meters above sea level. The

[2] Główny Urząd Statystyczny, Rocznik Statystyczny 1968 (Warsaw: 1969), Tables 7 and 8, p. 3.

16

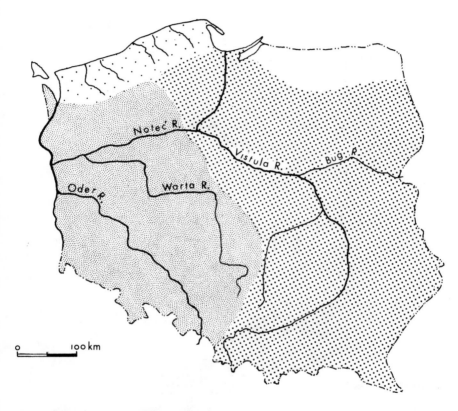

FIGURE 2.2.: MAJOR DRAINAGE BASINS OF POLAND

Source: Państwowy Instytut Hydrologiczny i Meteorologiczny, Warsaw

17

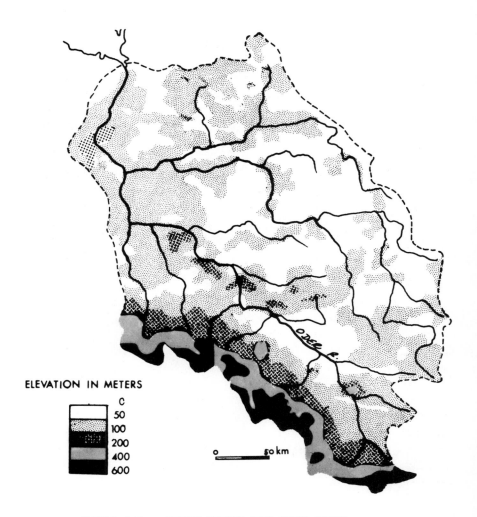

ELEVATION IN METERS

	C
	50
	100
	200
	400
	600

o   50 km

FIGURE 2.3.:   RELIEF WITHIN ODER RIVER BASIN

Source: Janiszewski, Atlas Geograficzny Polski, 1959

mountainous river valley is narrow and winding with steep slopes, particularly where the old rock is well exposed. The whole region has an appearance of being developed partially through diastrophism and partially through erosional processes. Thus in the extreme southern portion of the basin the Oder flows predominantly in a valley which is structurally controlled, whereas in the northern portion the structural control is less apparent.

As the Oder River enters the Moravian Gate it makes an almost 90 degree turn, changing direction from southeastward toward the northeast. The valley widens from two to three kilometers in width and due to deposition, as a result of drastic reduction in velocity, it becomes swampy in some parts while alluvial terraces are clearly noticeable in other parts of the same general area. As the Oder proceeds in a general northerly direction through the Moravian Gate toward the city of Ostrava, the Oder Mountains are located on the river's left bank and the Middle Beskidy, which are a part of the Carpathian Mountains, are on the right bank. With the passage of the Oder through the Moravian Gate, the valley acquires an entirely new appearance. Here, the sizable valley was carved by the confluence of four mountain streams, the Oder, Ostrawica, Olsza, and Opawa, flowing southwest from the Sudeten Mountains of Bohemia.[3] By contrast, the right bank tributaries are few in the southern portion of the drainage basin and their total discharge to the Oder, in comparison, is small.

As the Oder River enters the broad plain it changes its direction and is prevented from pursuing its northeasterly flow by the Silesian rise which towers to the north of the valley. It appears that the Oder River valley in this region, once again, is structurally controlled. These rapid changes in the directional flow, however, are not entirely due to protrusions and the structure of the old rock

[3]
Jerzy Kondracki, Geografia Fizyczna Polski (Warsaw: Państwowe Wydawnitstwo Naukowe, 1967), p. 126.

19

formations. In many instances, particularly in the north, changes which took place in the landscape during the glacial period greatly influenced the directional flow of all European rivers draining to the Baltic Sea including the Oder. In this respect, conditions for the Oder River were rather exceptional because the valley became mantled by an ice mass of both the Southern Polish and the Middle Polish Glaciations.[4] The northern section of the Oder drainage basin was not developed prior to the first interglacial period. After the Baltic depression had been carved out by the continental glacier and filled in the post-glacial period, only then the northern section of the basin was developed. Thus, where the river has an east-west or northwestern orientation, this directional flow was imposed when the stream became temporarily blocked from its northerly flow by an ice sheet during the glacial period.

In summary, one can say that the overall northerly directional flow of the Oder River was imposed by orogenesis whereas the deflection from this flow into a westerly direction arose from the periodical halting of the receding continental glacier. The existence of former river valleys or "pradoliny" (e.g. Głogów-Barycz, Wrocław-Bremen, marginal valleys) well support this view.[5]

Looking at the entire Oder River basin, shown in Figure 2.4., one can delimit three distinctive hydrographic regions.[6] The wide coastal belt which includes the Great Baltic End Morain extends from the Baltic Sea to the Warta-Noteć Rivers. This is a

[4]
Stanisław Szczepankiewicz, "Neo-Pleistocene Changes in a Large River Valley with the Oder as Example," Geografii Polonica, 1970, pp. 23-33.

[5]
Ibid., p. 25.

[6]
Jadwiga Orsztynowicz, "Udział Wód Podziemnych w Bilansie Wodnym Dorzecza Odry w Latach 1951-1960," Gospodarka Wodna, No. 4 (Warsaw: 1969), pp. 157-158.

region which can be characterized as having a surplus of water.

The triangular shaped area to the south of this coastal belt, extending from the Warta-Noteć Valley to the eastern edge of the Oder River valley, is an area of water deficit. This deficit of surface water is caused, not only by climatic conditions, but also by the constantly increasing industrial demands. The already existing water shortage is greatly aggravated by the ever-increasing consumption of large quantities of water by the industrial complexes of Upper and Lower Silesia, Łódz, and Warsaw. The third area, which is an area of water surplus, includes the valley of the Oder and extends southwestward to the Czechoslovakian border. This is an area of piedmont preceding the Sudeten Mountains. Due to the fact that the Oder from Ostrava to Głogów parallels the Sudeten Mountains for approximately 300 kilometers, the river in this area is supplied with an ample amount of water in the spring from melting snow in the mountains and orographic precipitation with a maximum in June.

The middle Oder River basin, as it has been pointed out, sandwiched between two areas of water surplus, is an area of water deficit. Fortunately, the segment of the Oder River most affected by the low water level is relatively small. The apex of the triangle extends from the point where the Nysa-Łużycka enters the Oder to Kostrzyń, where the Warta another tributary empties its waters, an approximate distance of 75 kilometers. The broad base of the triangle lies to the east of the river valley. Nevertheless, the extremely low water level in the late summer and early fall greatly encumbers navigation in the middle segment of the Oder as it cannot permit barges of 500 or 1,000 ton displacement, which can freely navigate in the Gliwice Canal and the lower section of the river, to pass through the upper and middle Oder during the low water stage.[7]

7
  Władysław Magiera, Ekonomika Transportu Wodnego (Żeglugi Śródlądowej), Wyższa Szkoła Ekonomiczna w Szczecinie Nakładem Państwowego Wydawnictwa Naukowego (Wrocław: 1951), p. 10.

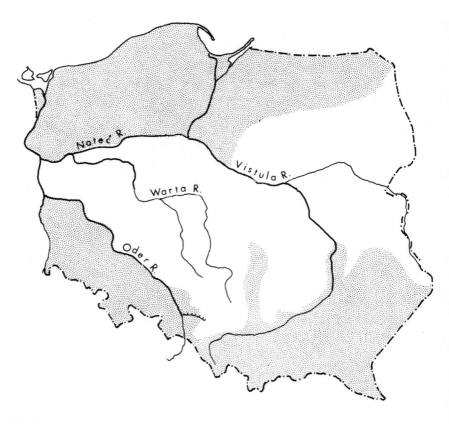

Nałęc R.

Vistula R.

Warta R.

Oder R.

AREA OF WATER DEFICIT

AREA OF WATER SURPLUS

FIGURE 2.4.:   SURFACE WATER BALANCE IN POLAND

Adopted from A. Tuszko

22

An additional obstacle to navigation are the spring floods associated with the melting of ice and the damming-up at the mouth of the rivers. As one can see, the general direction of Polish rivers is north-south. This direction coincides with the general warming trend in the spring. Consequently, with higher temperatures in the south and lower in the north, the danger of flooding increases as the water and ice begins to flow in the upper reaches of the rivers while the mouths, on many occasions, are still frozen solid. The Vistula is particularly susceptible to spring floods while in the Oder valley major catastrophic floods are very rare. The difference in the regime of these two major rivers, however, is largely due to the fact that the Oder has relatively few tributaries originating in the mountains while the Vistula has numerous such tributaries. By the same token, the mountainous part of the Oder basin, the Sudeten Mountains, on the average receive less precipitation than the Tatra and Carpathian Mountains, which are a sizable part of the Vistula River basin.

The committee of the Polish Academy of Science investigating fluvial problems and the other water requirements of Poland declared that the need for water in the Oder Basin is most pronounced.[8] The acute shortage of ground and surface water in the Oder River basin can be demonstrated by means of comparison with several European river flows. The annual flow of the Vistula at its mouth can rise up to 32km^3, while the Oder can attain at its maximum 18km^3. By comparing this with the Rhine's annual flow of 74km^3 and the Danube's 195km^3, the scanty discharge of the Oder River can be underscored.[9]

[8]
Aleksander Tuszko (ed.), Zarys Planu Perspektywicznego Gospodarki Wodnej w Polsce No. 8371, P.A.N. (Warsaw: 1968), p. 107.

[9]
Stanisław Skorowski, Geografja Gospodarcza Polski (Warsaw: Wydawnictwo Naukowe, 1939), p. 45.

What characterizes the Oder, however, from
a hydrological point of view, is not the small
annual quantity of water discharged but the rather
considerable seasonal fluctuations in the levels of
water. The level of water during the navigable
season may range from the flood stage to
catastrophically low levels. This immense variation
in the water levels not only makes navigation
extremely difficult and hazardous but it also
threatens the already existing meager supply of
water needed by the growing industry and urban
places within the area. Particularly along the
upper and middle river course, in the area of high
industrial concentration, a shortage of water
for industrial use could have serious economic
consequences. In addition, extension and
intensification of agriculture since 1960 within
the Oder Basin presents an additional demand for
water, thus greatly aggravating an already
existing problem.

From the point of navigability of the Oder,
a very important factor is the stages of middle
and low water levels in each month during the
navigation season. During a year the stages of
water are quire different, they range from low
water to high water. The analysis of the hydraulic
characteristics of the Oder River reveals that the
causes for seasonal fluctuations in the water
level are numerous and very complex ones.
Nevertheless, the single most important set of
causes for low water level is climatic. The
prolonged drought in the late summer and early fall,
typical for north central Europe, causes the
water to fall very rapidly, where with the spring
thawing of snow and ice and the June maximum
precipitation, the Oder approaches the dangerous
stage of flood. In the early spring, the Oder
floods due to ice jams accumulating in the river
channel. A corollary to the climatic reason as
to why the Oder's water level oscillates between
these two extremes is the fact that the middle and
lower portion of the river from Bedzin to
Szczecin, a distance of 478 kilometers, has

24

a small form ratio with an average slope of only 0.16 percent.[10] The maximum discharge of water is during the spring, caused by the thawing of snow and ice, and during the early summer, which is in turn caused by the rapid downpour of rain. Although the summer peaks of flow are more rapid than the spring peak flow, they are of a significantly shorter duration. Periodically the water cannot be contained within the banks which causes overbank flooding and creates a flood stage. In the present century two major floods were noted, July 2, 1903, and in the middle of September, 1938.[11]

To provide the necessary flood control and to help maintain minimum guaranteed depths of the navigable channel, a series of retention reservoirs shown in Table 2.2. and Figure 2.5. are located within the Oder River basin in the territory of Poland. In addition to the reservoirs on the territory of Poland, in Czechoslovakia and East Germany several new projects are under consideration in connection with the proposed construction of the Oder-Danube Canal.[12]

Characteristics of the Oder River Hinterland
The directional flow of the river and its relative location, in respect to the economic landscape of the country, is indicative of what role the river will play as an artery of transportation. The basic assumption here is that the demand for river transport, as of any other mode of transportation, is a derived

---

[10]
   Form ratio can be defined as depth divided by width which can be stated in fraction, e.g., 1/100 meaning that the stream channel is 100 times as wide as it is deep.

[11]
   Andrzej Grodek (ed.), Monografia Odry (Poznań: Instytut Zachodni, 1948), p. 250.

[12]
   Kazimierz Puczynski, "Kanał Odra-Dunaj," Gospodarka Wodna, Nr. 6 (June, 1968).

TABLE 2.2.

RETENTION RESERVOIRS WITHIN THE ODER RIVER BASIN

Location	Stream	Total Capacity of Reservoir in Million Cubic Meters
1. Dzierzno	Kłodnica	48.4
2. Dzierzno	Kłodnica	37.1
3. Jarnoltowek	Złoty Potok, Rudawa Obsobloga	2.4
4. Turawa	Mała Panew	98.5
5. Międzygorze	Wilcza	0.8
6. Stronie Śląskie	Morawa	1.3
7. Otmuchów	Nysa Kłodzka	128.0
8. Lubachów	Bystrzyca	8.0
9. Wojcieszów	Kaczawa	1.1
10. Swierzawa	Kamienny Pot.	1.7
11. Zarek	Nysa Szalona	5.0
12. Bukówka	Bóbr	2.4
13. Krzeszów I	Zadrna	---
14. Krzeszów II	Zadrna	0.9
15. Myślakowice	Łomnica	3.3
16. Malinnik	Malinnik	4.4
17. Cieplice Sl.	Sokon W.	6.2
18. Siedlęcin	Bóbr	0.5
19. Wrzeszczyn	Bóbr	1.8
20. Pilchowice	Bóbr	50.0
21. Mirsk	Chmieleńska W.	3.5
22. Złotniki Łubańskie	Kwisa	12.0
23. Leśna	Kwisa	15.0
24. Głębinów	Nysa	110.0
25. Racibórz	Oder	250.0

Note: In addition, there are five small reservoirs on the territory of Czechoslovakia.

Source: Andrzej Grodek (ed.), Monografia Odry (Poznań: Institut Zachodni, 1948), p. 480; Marian Miklowski, "Aktualna budowa zbiornika wodnego w Raciborzu i Kanału Żeglugowego," Gospodarka Wodna, XXVIII, Nr. 7 (July, 1968).

FIGURE 2.5.: RESERVOIR SYSTEM OF THE ODER RIVER

Source: Based on the data obtained from Okregowy Urzad Dyrekcii Dróg
Wodnych Office in Wrocław

demand which arises from economic conditions within the hinterland.[13] Thus, by providing accessibility within the hinterland, the river, by meeting the quantitative and qualitative demand imposed by the economy, will allow one to judge the river's importance and performance in absolute or relative terms to that particular region.

The directional flow and relative location of the river in relation to the economic landscape is of paramount importance irrespective to the physical conditions of the river and its state of navigability. This point can be exemplified by looking at the great Siberian rivers, great from the degree of volume of water and length of territory through which they flow. In spite of the hydrological and physical attributes of the mighty Siberian rivers, the directional flow of the Ob, Yenisey, and Lena is northward, emptying their waters into the frozen Arctic Ocean. An additional negative factor is that these rivers in the middle lower reaches flow through sparsely settled wilderness and economically underdeveloped regions. Thus their status and their significance as an artery of transportation in the Soviet transportation system, in spite of the physical attributes, is relatively small. The axis of the economic landscape in Siberia has an east-west orientation and the desired direction of movement of goods and people coincides with the economic landscape. Thus these negative factors, such as directional flow and the relative location of Siberian rivers in respect to the distribution of natural resources and location of industry and markets make these rivers, as arteries of transportation, relatively insignificant. On the other hand, relatively minor rivers with less advantageous physical conditions may have great economic importance as arteries of transportation because they flow through the axis of industrial regions of great importance to

[13]
  The term hinterland is used here to denote an undelineated area within the river's sphere of economic influence.

28

the nation's economy. From the point of navigability, the Ohio and Rhine Rivers are less than can
be desired, however, no one can dispute their
great economic importance as arteries of transportation.

Although the Oder River watershed embraces
portions of three sovereign and independent states,
the German Democratic Republic, Czechoslovakia,
and Poland, of these the most directly affected
and presented an economic asset by the river is
Poland and, to be more specific, the województwa
Katowice, Opole, Wrocław, Zielona Góra, and
Szczecin.

The magnitude and the relative importance of
a river to the national economy, whether this
is measured by the tonnages carried, the type of
commodity moved, or its share in the make-up of
the total transportation system, will depend on
economic conditions within the hinterland through
which it flows. If the regions of which the
hinterland is made up are considered to be poor,
underdeveloped, and relatively unimportant to a
nation's economy, thus generating small shipments,
then no matter what the estimated optimum capacity
or physical attributes of a particular river, it
has ultimately to be considered relatively
unimportant to that economy. However, as the
hinterland and economic conditions within the
hinterland change, the importance of the river will
also tend to change. Therefore it is imperative
that a brief history of the economic development
of the area should be included.

In the middle of the nineteenth century,
Upper Silesia held great promise of developing
into a most important industrial center. At that
time, it was described as equal to the one of
England and foremost on the continent of Europe.
Nevertheless, Upper Silesia, prior to World War I,
did not constitute one economic unit. The Upper
Silesia coalfields and industrial area were
divided between Prussia, Russia, and Austria. Both
Russia and Austria held in miniature the resources

and potentialities which the Prussians enjoyed in full measure in Upper Silesia.[14]

In looking at the Pre-World War I hinterland of the Oder River, one gains an instinctive impression that the Oder as "the river of the German East" had only secondary importance to the Reich's economy. The reason for Germany's inability to utilize the Oder to a greater advantage as an artery of transportation was not exclusively geographic in nature, but it also had politico-economic connotations. In spite of the fact that Upper Silesia, until 1853, produced over 40 percent of the total Prussian pig iron output, at the time of intense industrialization of Germany, disproportionally large amounts of capital were allocated to the western regions of Germany.[15] The nonferrous metal industries of Upper Silesia were, except at the beginning of the century, less important than either the iron, steel, or the coal, and their share in the total production of the region tended to decline during the century.[16]

The Ruhr area, at the end of the nineteenth century, became the most important single German industrial region. Justification for this policy was the necessity of completing the unification of Germany politically, thus of binding the western regions economically to the rest of Germany, as it was feared, not without justification, that the Saarlanders and Rhinelanders might find greater economic benefits with neighbors to the west than with the rest of Germany. German planners hoped that

14
Kazimierz Popiołek, "Koncetracja i Centralizacja Produkcji w Górniczo-Hutniczym Przemysle Górnego Śląska w Połowie XIX Wieku," Kwartalnik Historyczny, P.A.N., LXIII, Nr. 405 (1956), pp. 265-267.

15
L. Beck, Geschichte Des Eisens, IV, Hermann Fuchner, "Geschiche Des Schlesischen Berg-Und Huttenwesens in Der Zeit Friedrichs Des Grossen, Friedrich Wilhelms II und Friedrich Wilhelm III," Z.F.D. B.H.U.S., XLVIII (1900).

16
E.A. Smith, The Zinc Industry (London: Longman's & Company, 1918), pp. 10-18.

locating the major portion of heavy industry along the Rhine would assure their allegiance in two ways: one, creating incompatibility by developing competition between these regions and French heavy industry which lies immediately to the west and, secondly, by offering to the Rhineland exclusive German markets which lie to the east protected by high tariffs.

This process of concentration of capital in the western regions of Germany, which continued to the outbreak of World War II parallel with the migration of population, had an overall effect of increasing national revenue in the western regions and lowering it in the east.[17] The fact that the eastern regions of Germany remained predominantly agricultural, generating low traffic densities, made the Oder River somewhat a less important artery of transportation, becoming subject to administrative neglect. The main reason for German neglect of the Oder waterway in the interwar period was both the political and economic status of Upper Silesia for which the river is a natural outlet.

An additional reason for German economic neglect and virtual abandoning of the Oder waterway lies in the sphere of physical geography. In the interwar period, three states, Czechoslovakia, Germany and Poland shared the basin of the Oder River. As one can see in Figure 2.6., however, the Oder's major tributaries, the Warta and the Noteć, representing 70 percent of its network system which links the Oder with the Vistula, are flowing from the east.

The partition of the Upper Silesia after World War I, as shown in Figure 2.6., despite the precautions taken to preserve some functional unity, was a cruel blow to its industry and, consequently, to the transportation on the Oder. Germany retained approximately 600 square kilometers of the coalfield area of 2,800 square kilometers which she possessed

17
    Franciszek Ryszka, "Kapitał Monopolistyczny Na Górnym Śląsku i Formy Jego Polityki," Przegląnd Zachodni (1952), pp. 203-265.

before the partition and Germany's estimated reserves of coal were reduced from about 57.8 to about 8.7 million tons.[18]   German losses in coking coal in Upper Silesia were yet more severe.   This dismemberment of industrial units, which had been pieced together during the previous half century and had grown slowly into a functional unit, appeared to be a great tragedy.

The Geneva Convention had provided for the unrestricted movement of raw and part-finished materials across the boundary for a number of years.   It was intended that this period should be used in each country to prepare for the full rigors of national competition and spatial realignment.

The division of Upper Silesia undoubtedly dealt more harshly with the part which remained German than with the part that passed to Poland.   Firms which were left entirely on the German side of the boundary were relatively small and were dependent on coal from the other side.   It had been assumed that Germany and West Upper Silesia would be obliged to import coal in considerable quantity from Polish Upper Silesia. Provision had been made in the Geneva Convention and Poland's commercial policy was based on this assumption but such expectations proved ill-founded.   West Upper Silesia was in fact ill-placed to continue production of iron and steel.   None of the few small iron mines of Upper Silesia were left in Germany, local supplies of coking coal were inadequate, and the rising labor cost made the area unattractive as a producer of iron and steel.   The western part of Upper Silesia was a high-cost producer and the prices were above that of the Ruhr.   Its market was restricted to eastern Germany where it was insulated to some extent by distance from central and western Europe. The German part of Silesia was losing the battle against the competition of the Ruhr and Rhineland.

---

[18]
   Norman J.G. Pounds, The Upper Silesian Industrial Region (Bloomington: Indiana University Press, 1958).

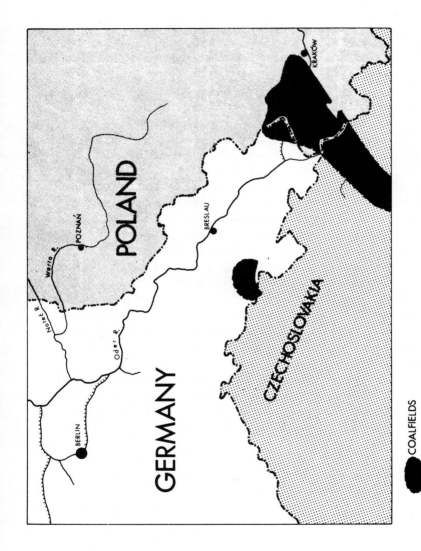

COALFIELDS

FIGURE 2.6.: PRE-1939 ODER RIVER HINTERLAND

33

The problem of transport cost was dominant. The
German railways permitted iron ore to be carried at
preferential rates, but this did not suffice to off-
set the immense advantage conferred on the Ruhr,
Silesia's chief rival, by the facility of cheap water
transport.

The Oder had, indeed, been made navigable under
normal weather conditions for medium-sized barges but
the Klodnitz Canal, which joined the industrial area
with the Oder River port of Koźle, remained as it had
been left after the improvements made in the 1880's.[19]
In the 1920's the traffic on the canal was only a
minute fraction of that carried on the Oder itself.
Clearly, the advantages of water transportation could
be achieved only if barges could be brought to Gliwice
itself. The completion of the Adolf Hitler Canal in
1940, along the route of the old Klodnitz Canal, was
designed to achieve this end. Indeed, the German
planners envisioned a veritable network of canals
linking the Oder with the Vistula, Danube, and Upper
Elbe.[20] The completion of such a project would certainly have lowered the costs and widened the market
for the industries of Upper Silesia. The Second
World War came before the effects of the opening of
the new canal had been fully apparent but there were
indications before 1939 that industries might be re-
located and revived along the banks of the new
waterway.[21]

In spite of this physical disadvantage to the
Germany economy, the Oder would have been able to
attain its greater economic scope if it had been
given the chance to serve its neighboring

[19]
In place of the old Klodnitz Canal, a new canal, the Adolf Hitler Canal,
was engineered and completed in 1940. It was renamed the Gliwice Canal
after World War II.

[20]
Hans F. Zeck, Die Deutsche Wirtschaft und Sudosteuropa (Leipzig: 1931),
p. 81.

[21]
"Oberschlesien als Standort einer Eisenschaffenden Industrie,"
Vierjahresplan, V (1941), pp. 472-476.

territories situated on the right bank of the river where the nucleus of Polish heavy industry began to develop. Instead, however, the political boundary between Germany and Poland, reinforced by the traditional hostilities between these two nations, prevented greater use of the Oder River by Polish industry, in spite of the great need for cheap water transportation.

Within the boundaries of 1939, the Oder was a waterway disinherited economically as it did not constitute a continuous artery of transportation throughout its entire length. Instead, the Oder was divided, from the point of traffic densities and direction, into three segments with nearly all its shipments moved in one directional flow toward the district of Greater Berlin.

The first segment, which extended from Western Upper Silesia to the Oder-Spree Canal, had a canalized section extending from Koźle to Wrocław, with the remaining portion of the river running freely. Coal, the most important commodity in terms of tonnages, 95 percent in this segment, was moved from Western Upper Silesia through the Oder-Spree Canal to a destination in the area of Greater Berlin.[22]

The middle segment of the Oder River, the sector between the Oder-Spree and the Oder-Havel Canals, was the least suitable for navigation and was a virtually unused portion. The reasons for this section not being used were not entirely due to the low water level as a result of climatic conditions and lack of navigational improvements, but rather due to the preferential direction of movement of commodity as dictated by the economy.

The third segment, the smallest of the three, extending from the point where the Havel Canal enters the Oder to Szczecin, was used as a connecting link

[22]
Engineer Research Office, Navigable Waterways of Germany (Strategic Intelligence Branch, Military Intelligence Division, VIII, August, 1944), pp. 34-100.

between the industrial region of Greater Berlin and
the port of Szczecin. In fact, Szczecin became the
economic outlet for the Berlin area. Manufactured
goods from Berlin destined to East Prussia and other
Baltic ports moved via the Oder-Havel Canal and lower
Oder to Szczecin. German statistics show that in
1938, out of a total of 17,658 ships navigating the
Reich's inland waterways, only 3,274 navigated within
the Oder region.[23]

In fact, the Oder River was never used as an
artery of transportation in its full meaning of the
term but rather individual segments of the Oder were
used in the preferable east-west movement. Thus, if
one looks at the pattern of flow of raw materials
and agricultural products in the eastern regions of
Germany this pattern shows convergence on Greater
Berlin. The industrial might of Germany was not
located along the Oder, which would in turn necessitate axial movement of freight along the entire
river, but in the west. Consequently, the eastern
regions were considered, in comparison to the
western regions, economically less developed and
primarily agricultural in nature.

The analysis of the total carrying capacity of
the German inland fleet by river basin shows in
Table 2.3. that more than 83 percent of the vessels
ranged between 201 and 600 tons capacity. This can
be compared with the Rhine which shows that almost
70 percent of its tonnages, in 1938, were carried in
vessels ranging between 901 and 1,401 and larger ton
capacity. Size of movement units, in this case size
of barges, not only reflects the technical limitations of the way but also mirrors the relative
economic importance of the way to the total
circulation system.

In summary, the Oder did not flow along the
desired direction of movement but across it. Thus
navigation on the Oder was the reflection of poor
economic conditions in which the regions of the east

[23]
  Engineer Research Office, XXXVII, pp. 11-12.

TABLE 2.3.

TOTAL CARRYING CAPACITY OF THE GERMAN INLAND FLEET BY RIVER BASINS AND
BY TONNAGE CLASSES (JANUARY 1, 1938)

Carrying Capacity (in tons)	E. Prussia Waterways %	Oder Area %	Mark Bran-denburg %	Elbe Area %	N.W. German Waterways %	Rhine Area %	Danube Area %	Saar %	German Reich %
21-50	1.3	0.4	0.7	0.5	1.3	0.2	0.2	---	0.5
51-200	18.6	4.4	3.2	3.2	6.1	2.4	4.4	0.9	3.8
201-350	31.6	29.7	53.6	7.3	6.5	3.8	1.6	90.4	15.4
351-600	41.3	52.9	29.7	30.3	16.4	7.2	5.7	8.7	23.6
601-900	7.2	12.5	11.1	42.2	38.2	16.7	81.9	---	24.3
901-1400	---	0.1	1.7	16.3	31.5	40.1	6.2	---	21.7
1401 & over	---	---	---	---	---	29.6	---	---	10.7

Source: Engineer Research Office, Navigable Waterways of Germany (Strategic Intelligence Branch, Military Intelligence Division, XXXVII, August, 1944), Table 37-IV, p. 14.

had been left by German planners. In comparison, it
can be shown that in response to economic inducements
and demand, great care had been taken to provide for
navigational improvement on the Rhine and Elbe.[24]
One can say that the German state, within its 1939
boundaries, did not allot the Oder an important
economic role largely because Upper Silesia for which
the Oder was a natural outlet did not represent one
economic unit. The German portion of Upper Silesia,
as shown in Figure 2.6., was small and insignificant
in comparison to eastern Poland and Czechoslovakia.
Poland, however, with its lion's share of Upper
Silesia did not have accessibility to the Oder. The
need for cheap water transportation was paramount and
Polish planners, before World War II, proposed a
canal which would link Upper Silesia with the maritime port of Gdynia. This proposed canal was to be
located approximately 100 kilometers east of the
Oder and largely parallel to it.

In the geographic and political system of central
Europe in the Post-World War II period, the place
the Oder occupies, as a link in the transportation
system, is dissimilar to that of the prewar period.
The river has become an important waterway in the
service of Poland and, to a lesser extent, the German
and Czechoslovakian economies as a result of politico-
economic changes within the regions.

The westward movement of Poland's boundary to the
line of the Sudetens, the Nysa-Łużycka, and the lower
Oder has not only greatly increased the country's
industrial potential but also gave the Oder an
extensive and rich hinterland. Poland acquired
several industrial agglomerations along the foothills
of the Sudetens and important industrial centers
along the Oder River in Koźle, Opole, Wrocław, and
Szczecin. Coal resources were increased by

[24] Engineer Research Office, II, p. 6A and VI, p. 26B.

two-thirds with the acquisition of the Lower Silesian field at Wałbrzych and the German-held sector of Upper Silesia.[25]

The importance of the Oder to the Polish economy stems, in particular, from the river's relative location and its directional flow to the distribution of natural resources, population, and location of industry. Figure 2.7. shows the distribution of the major mineral resources in Poland and the relative location of the Oder to these resources. As one can see in Figure 2.7., nearly 90 percent of the river's entire basin is located in Western Poland in the area of the largest mineral concentration.[26] The Oder River, in its upper reaches, is connected by the Gliwice Canal to extensive coal, tin and lead deposits in Upper Silesia. The coal, copper, nickel, and chromium deposits of Lower Silesia are connected to the Oder by several railroad feeder lines at Wrocław. In the middle reaches, the Oder below Wrocław flows adjacent to extensive though little-developed lignite and copper deposits in the województwa of Wrocław and Zielona Góra. Only in the lower reaches, from the point where the Warta, the major tributary, joins the Oder to the Bay of Szczecin, are there no significant mineral deposits in close proximity to the river.

Perhaps more important than the actual increase in the wealth of natural resources accessible to the river is the unified control which has been established over the whole Upper Silesia. This in turn permits more effective use and economic development of the area. The Oder seems to be the natural outlet for the coal and industrial products of Upper and Lower Silesia.

---

[25] Franciszek Barcinski, "Bogactwa naturalne ziemodzyskanych i ich znaczenie gospodarcze dla Polski," Przegląd Zachodni, III (1947), pp. 12-30.

[26] Jan Kolipinski, "Rola Ziem Odzyskanych w Organizmie Gospodarczym Polski," Przegląd Zachodni, II (1946), pp. 511-521.

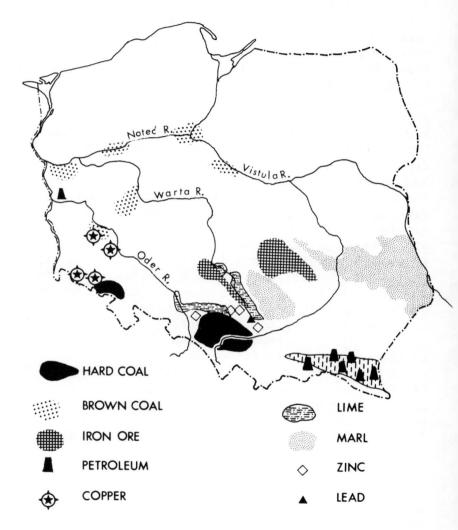

FIGURE 2.7.: DISTRIBUTION OF NATURAL RESOURCES

Source: Stanisław Leszczycki, ed., Zarys Geografii Ekonomicznej Polski, (Warsaw: Państwowe Wydawnictwo Naukowe, 1967), p. 16

40

In examining Figure 2.7. which shows the location of mineral resources, and Figure 2.8., showing the location of industry, one can see that the heaviest concentration of industry, known as Górnoslaski Okreg Przemysłowy, is in województwo Katowice and in the western part of województwo Kraków. In addition, a smaller industrial agglomeration, the Wałbrzych industrial region, is located in the southern part of województwo Wrocław. The areas surrounding the cities of Warsaw, Łódz, and Wrocław also show a fairly high percentage of industrial concentration. One can draw a diagonal line across Poland from Szczecin through Bydgoszcz, Warsaw, to Lublin which would separate the relatively industrialized west and southwest from an almost nonindustrialized northeast and east. The heavy predominance of Upper Silesia is apparent from examining Figure 2.8. One may delimit the industrial belt of Poland which reaches from województwo Kraków and includes województwa Katowice, Opole, and the southern portion of województwo Wrocław with its Wałbrzych district.

The importance of the Oder to the Polish economy may be underscored by showing that the Oder with its navigable tributaries is tied economically to approximately 34 percent of the Polish territory, inhabited by 40 percent of the population.[27] Furthermore, the river with the Gliwice Canal, in the segment from the Upper Silesian Industrial district to Wrocław, flows through the axis of the most industrialized part of Poland which produces slightly more than 50 percent of the total national output.[28]

In addition, important developments in agriculture and forestry in the area adjacent to the Oder can be noted. Particularly in województwa

[27] Główny Urząd Statystyczny, Rocznik Statystyczny 1968 (Warsaw: 1969), Table 7, p. 3.

[28] Władysław Misiuna, Rolnictwo na Ziemiach Zachodnich i Północnych (Poznań: Wydawnictwo Poznanskie, 1956).

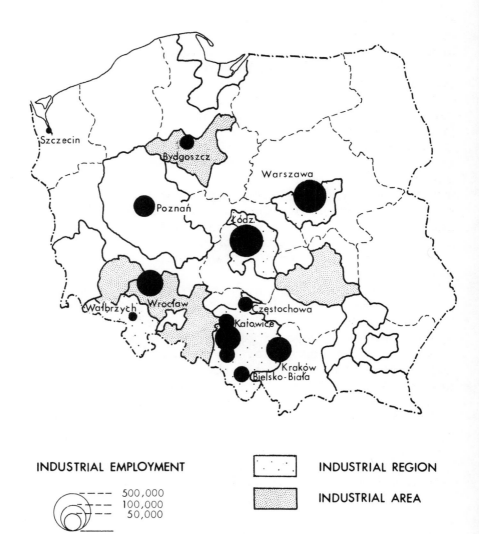

INDUSTRIAL EMPLOYMENT

500,000
100,000
50,000

INDUSTRIAL REGION

INDUSTRIAL AREA

FIGURE 2.8.:   DISTRIBUTION OF INDUSTRY

Source: M. Najgrakowski, "Zróznicowanie Przestrzenne Poziomów
          Uprzemysłowienia i Urbanizacji na Obszarze Polski," Miasto,
          Nr. 7-8, 1964

42

Opole, Wrocław, and some portions of województwo
Szczecin, the best agricultural yields in the country
are obtained in four types of grain. Consequently,
with the help of the Oder, the port of Szczecin, in
the 1950's, attained world importance as a grain
shipping port. Perhaps the relative importance and
the high degree of the exchange type of economic
activity within the area can be better understood by
pointing to the amount of traffic that is generated.
It has been estimated that within the Oder River basin
alone, as late as 1959, there was over 50 percent of
the railroad lines which carried approximately 70
percent of the nation's entire tonnage.[29] In recent
years, this relationship between województwa, in their
ability to generate traffic, hasn't changed
significantly.

[29]
  Teofil Lijewski, "Rozwój Sieci Kolejowej Polski," Dokum. Geogr. (1959),
pp. 15-48.

Chapter III

Navigational State of the River
Affecting Traffic Densities

The Oder River as an artery of transportation has
evolved in a setting comprising both environmental
and economic factors within the five regions through
which it flows. The river's ability, however, to
meet the demand for movement of goods and people
generated by the economic forces within this
hinterland depends to a large extent on the technological state of the waterway and its floating
equipment.

Any transportation system is made up of a
variety of components. A part of the system are the
vehicles, containers, in which goods and people are
transported. Another part of the system, as well,
are routes or ways, a geometric pattern of interconnected geographic locations. Motive power moves
the vehicles through the pattern of routes from one
place to another. In the case of the inland waterways, the routes to a large extent are provided by
nature, while their suitability for navigational
purposes depends on the directional flow, width, and
depth of the channel. The physical characteristics
of inland waterways will certainly determine the
type of floating equipment and the method of navigation that is used on that particular routeway.

Significant as components of any transportation
system are the assemblages of terminals. These
function as nodal points in the system, points of
accessibility in the network.

Therefore, the purpose of this chapter is to
analyze the composite structure of the Oder River as
an artery of transportation by analyzing the
individual components of the inland waterway such

GEOG 105
Test 2
February 28, 1990

Definitions and Listing

1. Define Dewpoint Temperature

2. What temperature and moistu
   with a continental tropical

3. Recalling the Kansas isohye
   annual precipitation receive
   that received in western Ka

4. List the three processes of
   these processes results in
   atmosphere? (4 pts.)

5. Define ITC (What it stands

as location and accessibility to river ports, depth of navigable channel, and type of floating equipment. The analysis of the structure will enable one to answer the question, whether the Oder constitutes a uniform and homogeneous way, capable of meeting both its quantitative and qualitative demands throughout its entire navigable length, or whether it has physical and technical limitations in way, vehicle, and accessibility which would greatly limit its usefulness as a continuous artery of transportation.

Location and Accessibility to River Ports

It is evident that early settlements along the Oder, functioning as ports, developed precisely at the points where river traffic converged or inter-changed with railroads and highway carriers. River ports, like any other terminals, an integral part of any transportation mode, can be looked at as nodal points where various modes and systems of transportation come together.

Along the Oder, spread over a distance of 636 kilometers, are located twenty-one ports and anchorages, twelve of which are active ports as shown in Figure 3.1. and two, Scinawa and Głogów, which are presently nonfunctioning. A closer examination of the topographic maps reveals that with few exceptions there is a uniformity in spacing of river ports along the Oder. The distance between ports is approximately 40 kilometers. This phenomenon perhaps may be analogous to Christaller's "central place" location of towns.[1] Here the spacing factor, of the points of accessibility, appears to be the fact that a commodity from the hinterland will move only a certain distance to a river port.

The fact that the ports along the Oder are on one bank or the other cannot be considered merely a matter of topographic chance. Rather, a review of historical data suggests that economic and political forces

---

[1]
Walter Christaller, Central Places in Southern Germany (Englewood Cliffs, New Jersey: Prentice-Hall, Inc., 1966), pp. 31-60.

45

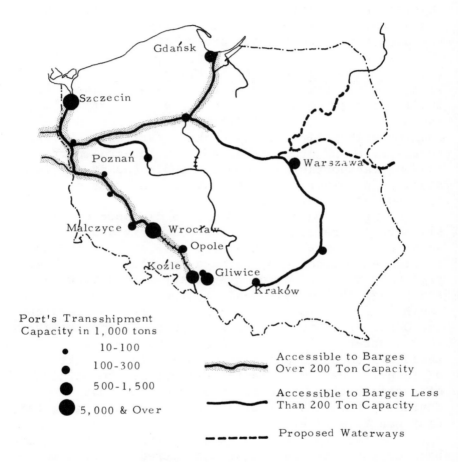

Port's Transshipment
Capacity in 1,000 tons

- 10-100
- 100-300
- 500-1,500
- 5,000 & Over

Accessible to Barges
Over 200 Ton Capacity

Accessible to Barges Less
Than 200 Ton Capacity

Proposed Waterways

FIGURE 3.1.:   INLAND WATERWAYS AND MAJOR PORTS OF POLAND

46

were at play in the locational decision of the Oder's ports. The location and spacing of towns and ports along the river largely depends on the function of the river itself. The river can be thought of as either a routeway along its axis, providing units and accessibility to the area, or it can be considered as a barrier to transportation and communication by physically separating places. Rivers in their unifying function, however, are not equally accessible throughout their entire course. Rather, their accessibility is limited to several points of entry and exit along their routeway. River ports or terminals perform the function of providing accessibility to both the hinterland and the river as a routeway.

In the case of the Oder, the river was historically both a barrier and a routeway. Since the tide of German settlement, commerce, and subsequent industrialization was moving from west to east, the initial towns were usually situated on the western bank. Some of these, such as Szczecin, Frankfort on Oder, and Wrocław, due to favorable economic and physical conditions, have persisted up to the present, developing into sizable cities. The Oder in its early function as an artery of transportation attracted traffic along its course by providing a relatively inexpensive form of transportation, so towns with anchorage facilities developed somewhat equally spaced on both banks of the river. The distance between these towns constituted a day's sailing time. But those, however, on the bank toward the freight source became dominant. For example, ports such as Koźle and Opole developed on the right bank of the Oder, becoming important bulk transferring ports, particularly loading ports, for Upper Silesia, an extensive and productive area lying east of the river. The ports of Malczyce, Wrocław, and Oława, developed on the left bank to serve Lower Silesia, an area lying to the south and southwest of the river.

Terminals are as important in the transportation picture as in line-haul. In fact, terminal problems often surpass those of line-haul in extent and complexity. The author here considers terminals as the sum total of facilities and their locale where road-haul traffic is originated, terminated, and/or interchanges before, during, or after the road-haul movement. These are the points where loads are assembled and/or broken down into small quantities. Such a grouping of facilities usually occurs at the end of a route but it also occurs frequently at one or more intermediate points along the route. It is only through these points, water terminals, that the river is accessible as an artery of transportation, as accessibility is not equal along the routeway's entire length.

Along the Oder from Gliwice to Szczecin twelve river ports are presently in use, including the maritime port of Szczecin. In total there are seven public terminals and twenty terminals exclusively owned and operated by industrial enterprises. The port facilities include not only those operated by water carriers serving the port such as piers, coal and ore docks, grain elevators, and other transfer facilities but also necessary local switching railroad, trucking concerns, towage, and storage warehouses. The type of traffic passing through a terminal has important effects on the operation and the facilities required. One may distinguish between commodity and traffic types and the peculiar needs of each.

Figure 3.2. shows two hypothetical models of terminal operations. Model "A" shows the movement of general cargo which includes a whole array of commodities ranging from manufactured goods, semi-processed goods, and fertilizer to agricultural products. The relatively small volumes and heterogeneous nature of the commodity requires extensive terminal operations and handling and it does not permit a high degree of mechanization in the transferring operation. One can say that this type of terminal operation is high labor intensive.

Model "B" shows the typical movement of bulk commodity. The homogeneity of the commodity and large volumes permit application of mechanization in loading and unloading operations. Here, transfer

48

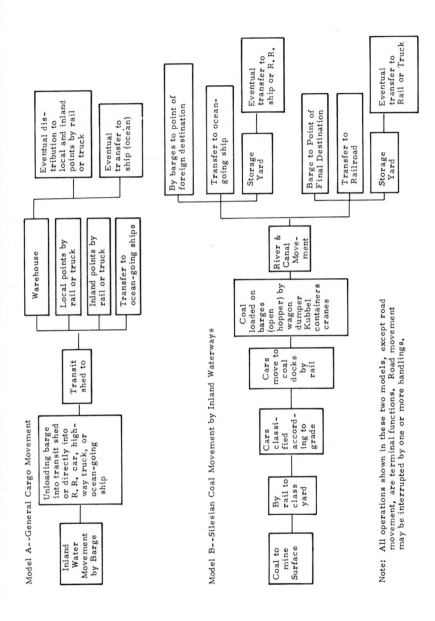

FIGURE 3.2.: MODELS OF TERMINAL OPERATIONS

Note: All operations shown in these two models, except road movement, are terminal functions. Road movement may be interrupted by one or more handlings.

49

operations are a relatively small percentage of the total cost of movement while transfer cost is relatively high in the case of general cargo movement.

In the case of the Oder's ports even the most superficial investigation reveals that not all the terminals have installations capable of handling commodity, especially when large quantities are concerned. A more detailed discussion of several Oder River ports below will exemplify these differences.

The port of Gliwice (see Figure 3.3.), typical of Model "B", situated on the eastern extremity of the Gliwice Canal, is the most modern of all the Oder ports. It is considered by Polish authorities to be capable of handling 6 million tons annually.[2] Lying on the western side of the Upper Silesian industrial district, it is the most convenient point for transshipment of coal from rail into barges. The fact that large quantities are involved here made it possible as well as economical, in spite of heavy capital outlay, to introduce a great deal of mechanization in coal hauling. The coal from the mines is shipped by "Kubbel" containers, which are lifted from railway wagons by four cranes of 17.5 tons, and emptied into open hopper type barges. It has been estimated by the Gliwice port authorities that by using "Kubbel" containers, the coal loading rate per crane is 330 tons per hour. Even if one takes the capacity of 250 tons per hour, as observed by the author, 2,000 tons can be handled in an eight hour working day. An additional six cranes, four of a capacity of 5 tons and two of a capacity of 7.5 tons, located in three basins make up the total mechanized transferring equipment for handling bulk commodity in the port.

The equipment and facilities, which are primarily designated to handle a large variety of small shipments, are old, inefficient, and seldom used. The third basin, designed to handle liquid fuels, is not in use

[2]
The estimate is based on the author's interview with the officials of the agency Żegluga na Odrze representatives in Gliwice.

FIGURE 3.3.: LOADING OF COAL IN PORT OF GLIWICE BY MEANS OF "KUBBEL" CONTAINERS

Photograph compliments of Żegluga na Odrze

51

for this purpose, at the present time, but is used as a receiving and storage depot for the lumber used at the mines. This brief description of the port's facilities, equipment, and methods in transfer operations underscores the primary function of the port at Gliwice which is coal loading.

The port of Koźle, another example of "B" type terminal operations like the port of Gliwice, plays an important role in the transshipment of Upper Silesian coal destined for domestic and foreign markets by inland waterways. Coal consigned for foreign export moves either by barges through a system of inland waterways to the point of destination, or it moves to Szczecin where it is loaded on an ocean-going ship for further shipment. Koźle is also a major unloading terminal of imported high grade Swedish iron ore for both Polish use and for transshipment consigned to the Ostrava-Karvina iron and steel complex in Czechoslovakia. The transshipment of coal takes place by the use of old and somewhat inefficient wagon dumpers. Czechoslovakian transit, iron ore and other raw materials, is unloaded at Koźle from barges into railroad cars for further shipment by rail to the point of destination. The annual capacity of the port of Koźle has been estimated by Polish officials to be approximately 1,000 thousand tons. With construction of the proposed canals, the Oder-Danube and the Oder-Vistula, the port of Koźle will assume a key national and international significance. Independently of this plan, in the period of 1970-1975, the planners envision expanding the terminal facilities in the port of Koźle to 7,000 thousand ton annual capacity which would also allow the use of modern floating equipment. Koźle will become a hub for two major inland water routes linking the Danube with the Baltic Sea and the Vistual, via the Oder and the Elbe, with the entire Middle and Eastern European inland waterway system.

The city of Wrocław has two ports. The port Miejski (city port, see Figure 3.4.) is an example of "A" type terminal operations especially equipped to handle an assortment of commodities originating or terminating locally in the surrounding areas and

FIGURE 3.4.: PORT MIEJSKI (CITY PORT)

Photograph compliments of Żegluga na Odrze

53

foreign shipments such as coal, building materials, raw materials for light industry, as well as a multiplicity of finished goods. The shore installations at this Wrocław port are old and are long overdue for replacement. The low estimated annual capacity of 760 thousand tons for Wrocław's port, Miejski, reflects perhaps the inefficiency of its old shore installations and the low priorities assigned by planners in the reconstruction of port facilities. Lately, however, with increased Polish participation in foreign trade via inland waters, the port Miejski is assuming greater significance as a point of transshipment.

Wrocław's second port is Popowice, an example of "B" type. It is equipped to handle bulk commodity, mainly Lower Silesian coal, for the thermoelectric power plant located in the vicinity (see Figure 3.5.). The unloading of coal at Popowice is fully automated. With the help of a conveyor the coal is brought directly to the plant.

Both ports of Opole and Malczyce, examples of "A" type terminal operations, handle general cargo. Here, shipments and the multiplicity of commodity handled do not lend themselves well to application of mechanization in cargo handling. By nature this type of transshipment operation is high labor intensive, thus costly. The port of Opole in recent years has begun to develop its own specialization by handling potash imported from East Germany destined for the local fertilizer plants. Both ports also service barges of the agency Żegluga Bydgoska. The total capacity of the ports of Opole and Malczyce is equal to 150 and 280 thousands tons, respectively.

An attempt was made above to exemplify briefly terminal operations of both "A" and "B" models in real content. Table 3.1. summarizes the major characteristics of the Oder River ports presently in use.

An analysis of Oder River ports reveals the emergence of a type of geographic division of labor between the ports. This emerging division of labor cannot be attributed to planned economy but, rather, it is a natural response to new economic and

54

FIGURE 3.5.: PORT POPOWICE (WROCŁAW)

Photographed by the author

locational forces operating within the Oder River
valley. The fact is that some of the ports are in
close proximity to the developing industrial complexes or sites of existing or newly discovered raw
materials. Therefore, one would expect that the port
would serve its most immediate area. Greater specialization of the river ports would simplify and
expedite the flow of commodities on the Oder in the
sense that a particular port would transship, load,
or unload only a certain type of commodity rather
than all types of commodities as has been the case up
to the present, which would in turn allow a greater
application of mechanized equipment.

With the increased specialization of the Oder
ports, the present convergence and pattern of railroad lines will also be subjected to change in order
to provide greater accessibility from the hinterland
to these ports. Here is an example of overlapping
and complementarity between modes of transportation.
At the present, there are only three main points of
convergence of railroad lines along the Oder River.
Several major trunk lines converge on the ports of

TABLE 3.1.

SUMMARY OF THE MAJOR CHARACTERISTICS OF THE ODER RIVER PORTS

Ports	Estimated Annual Capacity (1000 tons)	Location from Confluence in Km.	No. of Basins	No. of Cranes	No. of Wagon Tippers	Storage Area in 1000 Sq. M.	RR Track in Port Area (in Km.)	Primary Function
Gliwice	6,000	41.6	3	10	--	68.3	11.5	Loading coal-90%; unloading iron ore-5%
Koźle	1,100	96.0	3	6+	6	54.3	19.5	Loading of coal-80%; unloading iron ore (Transit Czech.)
Opole	150	155.0	1	2	2	0.8	8.6	General Cargo, Loading of Cement (Reserve for Gliwice & Koźle)
Oława	10	215.0	1	2	--	10.0	*	General Cargo
Wrocław	760	256.0	2	20	1	5.8	21.8	General Cargo

Note: * Not Available

Table 3.1. continued on page 57.

56

TABLE 3.1.

Continued

Ports	Estimated Annual Capacity (1000 tons)	Location from Confluence in Km.	No. of Basins	No. of Cranes	No. of Wagon Tippers	Storage Area in 1000 Sq. M.	RR Track in Port Area (in Km.)	Primary Function
Malczyce	280	304.8	2	3	2	0.4	4.8	General Cargo
Nowa Sól	40	430.0	1	2	--	*	*	Anchorage for tugs
Cigacice	50	471.7	1	1	--	27.0	1.3	Transshipment of grain, Winter quarters (Coaling Station)
Kostrzyń	180	615.3	2	*	--	*	*	End of line for deep draft tugs
Szczecin	7,000+	738.0	14	*	--	*	*	Unloading coal

Note: * Not Available

Source: Data obtained from the office of the agency Żegluga na Odrze, Wrocław, June, 1968.

57

Gliwice, Koźle, and Wrocław; consequently, these
developed into the great ports of the Oder River.
The major factor here that enters into consideration
is the location of natural resources in close proximity to these ports. They have become outlets for
the surrounding mining and manufacturing areas. For
example, the coal from the Upper Silesian mines is
most conveniently shipped by railroad to Gliwice or
Koźle for further shipment by inland waterways. The
cement from Sosnowce moves by railroad and then is
loaded on barges at Gliwice. The port of Koźle lies
at the intersection of the major lines connecting
Upper Silesia with Lower Silesia and Czechoslovakia
with Poland through the Moravian Gate.

The pressure on Wrocław as a major point of
transshipment from railroad to barge and vice versa
and as a primary inland water outlet for Lower
Silesia can be somewhat lightened. In the vicinity
of Wrocław there are numerous smaller ports such as
Oława, Brzeg Dolny, or Malczyce which are, at least
in actual kilometer distance, closer to the sources
of raw materials. Thus, in turn, they could divide
some of the burden between them which is now largely
borne by Wrocław's ports. Recent developments in
the area point to the fact that that is exactly what
is being done. For example, with the recent dis-
covery of the copper fields southwest of Głogów,
this presently dead port is being revitalized.

On the basis of field examination of the Oder
River ports and their terminal facilities, the author
has divided a simple functional classification of
the ports. This classification is based on the volume
of traffic and present and potential commercial
significance to the movement on the Oder, rather than
on the method of terminal operations. All Oder River
ports can be divided into four categories:

1) Commercial--Class I (with annual minimum
   capacity of 250 thousand tons)
2) Commercial--Class II (with annual capacity
   less than 200 thousand tons)
3) Service Ports (no commercial value, serving
   exclusively the needs of the navigation

58

agency "Żegluga no Odrze," e.g., fueling
stations, shipyards, etc.)
4) Winter Quarters (for floating equipment).

In the category of commercial Oder River ports of
Class I, one can include: Gliwice, Koźle, Wrocław-
Popowice, Wrocław-City Port, Malczyce, and Szczecin,
and the inland water port at Golecin. The commercial
Oder River ports of Class II are: Oława, Nowa Sól,
Cigacice, Kostrzyń, and ports on the river Warta such
as Poznań and Miedzychód. The separate category is
"Winter Quarters" which consists either of natural or
articificially constructed basins, guarded against
ice and flood. The commercial ports also perform
the function of winter quarters for the fleet.

The rapid growth in inland water cargo handled
by the Oder River ports in recent years has been a
reflection of the expansion of physical facilities
which has taken place during the period of reconstruction. Statistics show that in spite of the
sharp drop during the year 1955 in the amount of
cargo handled by the Oder port, inland water cargo
appears to be on the threshold of new major growth
and expansion. At the end of 1968, the total cargo
handled by all inland water ports in Poland was
5,314 thousand tons, 59 percent of which was handled
by Oder ports.[3] In spite of rapid growth, inland
water traffic since 1960, if one compares it with
railroad, intercity trucking, and ocean freight, is
still small business. Specialization is on the side
of inland water-bound cargo. While today it may
represent only an infinitesimal portion of the total
domestic freight movement, small increases will
represent major growth in the actual volume of river
cargo handled.

Varying Widths and Depths of the Navigable Channel
The navigation channel of the waterway constitutes one
of the most important and integral part of this

[3]
  Główny Urząd Statystyczny, Statystyka Żeglugi Sródlądowej i Dróg
Wodnych Sródlądowych, 1968, No. 48, Table 24 (Warsaw: 1969), p. 47.

transportation industry. Hence, this not only determines the methods of navigation but also loads which, in turn, determines the total capacity of the waterway. The performance of vessels and tows under different conditions of navigable channel is well demonstrated on the great waterways of the United States and Europe. The prospect for the optimum or less than optimum operation can be predicted only after consideration of the features of channel design such as depth, width, and its curvature that collectively results in a successful performance of the inland water fleet.

Channel alignment and dimensions which would permit tows or vessels to proceed with full loads and at a reasonable speed, allowing such tows or vessels to pass one another without difficulty, must be made available. The design of the navigational channel has to take into consideration total tonnages that are expected to be carried, the type of floating equipment, and the method of navigation that will be used on that particular section of the waterway.

To permit the successful passage of tows similar to those navigating on other European inland waters, the Oder system must have ample physical dimensions. The problem of providing a navigable channel of adequate dimensions on the Oder to permit barges of a minimum 500 ton displacement to navigate without difficulty along its entire length and, at the same time, be practical from an engineering standpoint is a difficult one. The present physical characteristics of the Oder River present serious obstacles. The most crucial and seldom attainable physical characterictic of Polish inland waterways is adequate depth. The necessary depth for navigation should be sufficiently provided in order that a fully loaded vessel of a given tonnage can freely navigate without danger. These ideal conditions exist when there is at least 50 centimeter clearance between the fully loaded vessel and the channel bed as lesser clearance would cause a drastic increase in propulsive resistance.

Equally important to navigation are the curvatures and the widths of the channel which in a sense largely determines the type of floating equipment

that can be used and the method of navigation. In
the case of the Oder River, its navigable channel has
numerous bends with a small arc which limits the
width and length of tows. In the channelization of
the river, the minimum permissible length of the
radius of the arc within the channel will largely
depend on the width of the channel. The authorities
in the field of channel design state that the radius
should not be smaller than four times the width of the
channel but, at the same time, should not exceed ten
times the width.

To illustrate how the width and the curvature of
the navigable channel relates to the navigation method,
one may cite an example. The physical characteristics,
particularly depths, on some sections of the Oder River
permit the length of a tow up to 500 meters. However,
the economy and safety of movement on the channel requires that the length of the arc of the channel
should at least be twice the length of the tow which
permit the easy movement and passage of two tows.
Therefore, ideally the minimum length of the arc
should be at least 1,000 meters. This length, however,
is not always possible to obtain with the channelization of the upper Oder. In restricted channels having
small radii of curvature, it may be necessary to
neglect considerations of towing resistance and
arrange tows in order to obtain sufficient steerability
to negotiate sharp turns.

The size and shape of the navigable channel has
a most pronounced influence on the performance of
floating equipment and its power requirements to
overcome propulsive resistance. Probably the best
direct comparison of traction to speed relation was
obtained in the experiments by Peters.[4] The average
values for pull needed at certain speeds were computed
and are indicated in graphical form in Figure 3.6.
The line was plotted in the graph below indicating the
approximate relation between average traction and
speed for barges in still water.

[4]
F. Peters, Bestimmung Der Leistung von Schleppzugen; Werf Rederei und
Hafen, XVI (1925), pp. 463-468.

61

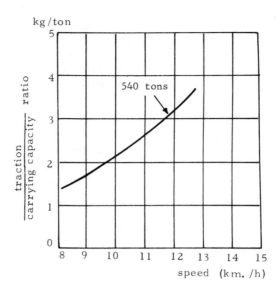

FIGURE 3.6.: RELATION BETWEEN TRACTION AND SPEED

The channel resistance to vessels increases rapidly as the speed of the vessel increases since the resistance varies nearly as the square of the speed.[5] The cost of additional power required for increasing the speed of the vessels above certain limits in restricted channels of given dimension may become greater than the advantage to be gained thereby. On the other hand, the provision of a larger channel would involve increasing the initial cost and annual maintenance which may not be fully justified by the benefits accruing from the possible reduced cost of transportation.

In 1923, Kempf published the results of experiments indicating the effect of channel depth to fleet draught ratio on resistance for Rhine barges.[6] In

[5]
Albert J. Dawson, "Design of Inland Waterway Barges," Transactions, Society of Naval Architects and Marine Engineers, LVIII (1950).

[6]
G. Kempf, "Economical Speeds in Shallow Water," Shipbuilding and Shipping Record, (June, 1924).

62

Figure 3.7. below, a curve was plotted for a constant speed of 15 kilometers per hour, indicating the speed loss or resistance increases in shallow water as compared with deep water speed and resistance, respectively.

For the purpose of comparison a line of constant speed was plotted in the figure below for barges combined into flotillas on American waters. It appears that the American curve indicates a higher resistance increase than the European. This can be explained perhaps by the differences in navigation method and by the difference in the type of floating equipment. The resistance of ship-shaped barges, as used in Europe, is affected by shallow depth to a lesser degree than the resistance of scow-ended barges used on American waters.[7]

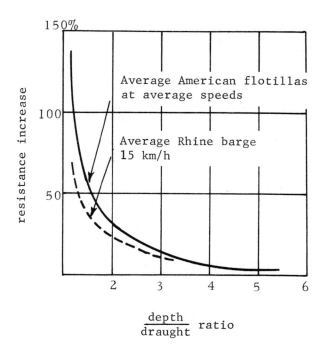

FIGURE 3.7.: EFFECT OF CHANNEL DEPTH AND VESSEL DRAUGHT ON RESISTANCE

7
 J.F. Allen and W.P. Walker, "Resistance of Barges in Deep and Shallow Water," Transactions of the Institution of Naval Architects (1948), pp. 154-167.

The relation of resistance to speed of vessels and tows, as demonstrated in these several experiments for subsequent use on inland waterways, indicates that high speeds for loaded tows on marginal waters, marginal from the point of width and depth of navigable channel, such as that of the Oder, are uneconomical and not warranted. Therefore, what is considered the proper dimensions of a channel involves many considerations. Conclusions reached in various investigations of restricted channels indicate that the cross-sectional area of the channel should be at least four and one-half times the submerged cross-sectional area of the loaded vessels or tows, the dimensions of which in turn are governed by the size of the locks.[8]

The Oder River system can be divided from the point of navigational conditions into four large sections: Gliwice Canal, Upper Channelized Oder, Middle shallow, freely flowing Oder and the relatively deep, freely flowing Lower Oder. Each of these sectors has its own distinctive idiosyncrasies and suitability for navigation. Table 3.2. below states the major fluvial characteristics such as width, depth, and gradient of each sector.

As one can see the Oder River varies greatly in its width and depth of navigable channel from one section of the way to the other. In the lower and upper sections of the Oder, the navigable channel is approximately 60 meters in width, the middle section, however, is considerably narrower, 40 meters. The most crucial characteristic of the navigable channel is the depths; as one can see in most cases, on the Oder, they are not nearly adequate. This picture becomes even graver if one points to the two extremes in the fluctuations of water level. The average low water level with high water extends over 215 days or 80 percent of the navigation period, while the middle water level with high water extends over 135 days or

[8]
U.S., Congress, House Document No. 178, Lake Erie and Ohio River Canal, 76th Congress, 1st Session, 1939.

TABLE 3.2.

CHARACTERISTICS OF THE ODER RIVER SYSTEM

Name of the Sector	Length in Km.	Maximum Permissible Barge Carrying Capacity	Depth of Navigable Channel		Average Gradient %	Width of Navigable Channel
			Min. Low Water Level	At Ave. Middle Water Level		
Gliwice Canal	40.6	1,000	300	350	----	40
Channelized Oder						
Racibórz-Koźle	45.0	170	50	120	----	40
Koźle-Brzeg Dolny	164.0	650	150	180	----	60
Freely-Flowing Oder						
Brzeg Dolny-Kostrzyń	356.0	500	120	170	0.28	40
Kostrzyń-Zatoń Górna	49.0	750	200	250	0.18	60
Zatoń Górna-Szczecin	73.0	1,000	250	300	0.03	60
Oder Tributaries						
Nysa-Łużycka (Gubin-Oder)	15.0	250	60	120	----	--
Warta (Konin-Prośna)	55.0	50	60	70	0.20	--
Warta (Prośna-Poznań)	105.0	200	70	120	0.17	--
Warta (Poznań-Noteć)	173.0	550	100	180	0.19	--
Warta (Noteć-Oder)	69.0	550	140	220	0.19	--

Source: Stanisław Andrjansk, Służba Liniowa Na Śródlądowych Drogach Wodnych (Warsaw: 1956), pp. 14-19.

50 percent of the navigational period. Consequently, due to the extensive fluctuation of high and low water levels during the navigable season, the controlling depths cannot be maintained along the entire length of the navigable Oder. The importance of the availability of adequate depths in the channel and over the lock sills cannot be underestimated as they determine the permissible drafts and the corresponding maximum tonnage for vessels.

The presently existing system of the Oder River is comprised of four distinctly different sectors suitable for navigation. Figure 3.8. shows the individual sectors and their respective make-up as a part of the inland water routeway.

The first section, the Gliwice Canal with a branch, the Kedzierzyn Canal, smallest of all four which is 40.6 kilometers long, 40 meters wide, and 3.5 meters deep, was designed to provide a water link between the coalfields and the center of heavy industry of Upper Silesia and the Oder. The canal is the newest and the most modern portion of the way in the entire Oder inland water system. Six twin chambers, 72 by 12 by 3.5 meters, with fully automated locks permit the passage of 750 ton barges. It has been estimated by the officials of the agency Żegluga na Odrze that in its present condition the Gliwice Canal's maximum annual capacity is 5.2 million tons with 24 hours a day operation. With the modernization and enlargement of the lock chambers this portion of the waterway between Gliwice and Koźle will be capable of carrying barges of a 1,000 ton load capacity.

The second sector, 164.0 kilometers long, extending from Koźle to Brzeg Dolny, 95.6 kilometers to 259.0 kilometers on the river, is the channelized portion of the Oder. In this sector the supposedly guaranteed depth is 1.5 meters, however, during a prolonged drought it is difficult to maintain even that minimum. Until recent years there has been no particular effort to standardize lock size on the Oder. This has resulted in a multiplicity of different types and sizes of locks. One may point out

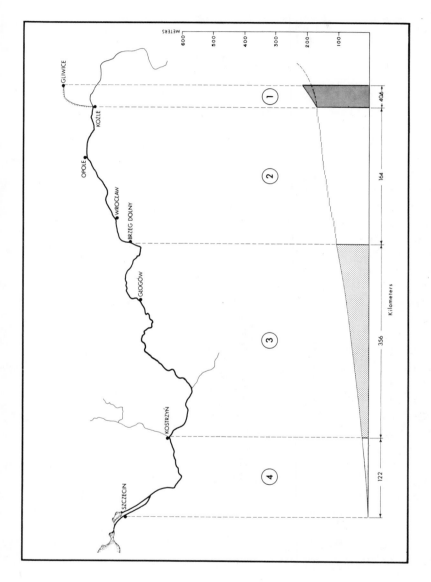

FIGURE 3.8.: PROFILE OF THE ODER WATERWAY

67

FIGURE 3.9.: GLIWICE CANAL BARGE B-500 PASSING THROUGH THE LOCKS

Photograph compliments of Żegluga na Odrze

68

FIGURE 3.10.: CHANNELIZED ODER, AT CITY OF WROCŁAW

Photographed by the author

69

that the efficiency of operation largely depends on the standardization of transportation equipment.

Table 3.3. lists and summarizes the major characteristics of locks on the channelized portion of the Oder. As one can see most of the lock chambers are relatively small. Only two chambers are capable of accomodating more than two barges in a single locking operation. Some of the locks from Koźle to Nysa-Kłodzka are very old and inefficient, being long overdue for replacement as several of these have been in use since 1895.[9] Theoretically, the maximum attainable speed on the channelized portion of the Oder waterway is listed as 12 kilometers per hour, however, this figure is very seldom achieved by even the most modern self-propelled barges. Numerous sandbars, lack of navigational aids, and obstructions make navigation on the channelized portion of the river hazardous. The objective of channelization of this portion of the Oder was to produce a minimum depth of 1.5 meters during the critical period of late summer and fall which would allow uninterrupted movement on the river. Unfortunately, this objective is not attainable without additional construction of retention reservoirs. In the mid-1970's it is hoped that a reservoir will be completed at Głebinów which will help to eliminate the summer interruption in navigation.

The freely flowing Oder from Brzeg Dolny to Swinoujscie, a total distance of 478 kilometers, can be divided into two sections, the 356 kilometer long middle Oder and the 122 kilometer long lower Oder.

The third sector, the middle Oder from Brzeg Dolny at 282.6 kilometers on the river to the confluence of the Warta River at 615.3 kilometers down the river, is the largest sector of the Oder waterway and the least suitable for navigation. Its shallow channel, poor quality of navigational aids, and terminal facilities greatly encumber navigation. In

9
 Andrzej Grodek (ed.), Monografia Odry (Poznań: Instytut Zachodni, 1948),
 p. 486.

TABLE 3.3.

LOCKS ON THE CHANNELIZED SECTOR OF THE ODER

Location	Km. on Oder from Source	Average Pool Level Above Sea Level		Difference Between Lower and Upper Pool (meters)	Lock Dimensions	
		Upper Chamber	Lower Chamber		Length (meters)	Width (meters)
Koźle (Januszkowice)	105.6	165.35	162.75	2.60	55.0	9.60
Stradunja	114.4	162.75	160.25	2.50	54.2	9.60
Krapkowice	122.9	160.25	157.65	2.60	55.0	9.60
Rogów Opolski	129.6	157.65	155.40	2.25	54.2	9.60
Ziemnice	137.4	155.34	153.24	2.10	55.0	9.60
Groszowice	144.6	153.30	151.20	2.10	55.0	9.60
Opole	150.4	151.20	149.10	2.10	54.2	9.60
Wróblin	157.5	149.10	146.70	2.40	55.0	9.60
Dobrzeń Wielki	164.0	146.70	144.45	2.25	55.0	9.60
Chroscice	168.3	144.45	142.70	7.75	55.0	9.60
Chroscice	168.5	142.70	140.45	2.25	187.0	9.60
Confluence of Nysa	180.4	140.45	138.10	2.35	187.2	9.60
Zwanowice	184.7	138.10	133.70	4.40	187.8	9.60
Brzeg	197.5	133.72	130.30	3.42	187.1	9.60
Lipki	208.1	130.29	128.31	1.98	187.2	9.60
Oława	213.4	127.96	124.17	3.99	55.0	9.60
Ratowice	227.2	123.70	121.14	2.56	187.8	9.60
Jeszkowice	231.7	121.10	117.70	3.40	225.1	12.00
Bartoszowice	245.0	117.70	114.60	3.10	187.7	9.60
Zacisze	250.3	114.60	112.30	2.30	186.1	9.60
Wrocław (Różanka)	254.0	112.30	110.00	2.30	196.2	9.60
Rędzin	261.6	109.80	106.06	3.58	203.1	12.00

Source: Data obtained from the office of Okręgowy Urząd Dyrekcii Dróg Wodnych, Wrocław, June, 1968.

FIGURE 3.11.: POPOWICE LOCK CHAMBER (WROCŁAW)

Photographed by the author

72

spite of the fact that the freely flowing Oder from Brzeg Dolny to Kostrzyń, at the confluence of the Warta, was regulated for low water, an attempt to maintain a minimum guaranteed depth of 125 centimeters during the late summer and early fall is not always possible. The slightest reduction of water level below the minimum guaranteed depth results in a temporary halt in navigation. These interruptions in navigation, due to low water levels, are quite frequent, lasting on the average of forty-five days annually during the course of the last decade.[10] Prior to the construction of the retention reservoirs at Otmuchów on the Nysa-Kłodzka and in Turów on the river Panwi, navigation in this sector was halted for even much longer periods. Regardless of these improvements, interruption of navigation in a single season, due to extremely low water levels, could last as long as 113 days.[11] Even though the minimum depth, 125 centimeters, of the navigable channel could be maintained throughout the season, barges operating in this middle section can only carry 65 to 70 percent of their tonnage capacity. As a fully loaded vessel has an average draught of 1.84 meters, to allow for full utilization of this section as a part of a continuous routeway from Koźle to Szczecin, a minimum depth of 2.34 meters has to be maintained throughout the season. At the present technological status, these depths are far from attainable in the middle sector of the Oder.

The fourth section of the waterway, the lower Oder from the confluence of the Warta at point 615.3 kilometers to the maritime port of Szczecin at 738 kilometers on the river, does not present major navigational problems. This is a section of relatively

10
   From the records of Zarząd Wodny (State Water Management Office), Nowa Sól, 1968.

11
   In 1953, the navigation season was interrupted, due to low water, 113 days and in 1969 by 102 days. From the records of the navigation agency Żegluga Na Odrze (Żhegluga na Odzhe).

deep water, with a minimum depth of two meters, as a result of the Oder receiving a large supply of water from its major tributary the Warta. Supplemental dredging of the channel in the lower section of the river below Zatoń Górna makes it possible for barges of 1,000 ton load capacity to freely navigate its waters. In the vicinity of Zatoń Górna, the lower Oder is divided into an eastern branch and a western branch, both of these branches are navigable. At the present time, however, the main navigable channel used by the Polish navigational agencies is the eastern branch of the Oder. The western branch, in turn, serves as the extension of the Hohenzollern Canal, linking Berlin with Szczecin via a system of inland waterways. In the vicinity of Gryfin and Krajnik, both branches of the Oder are connected by canals equipped with locks which permit easy passage of barges from one branch of the river to the other.

The analysis above reveals that the Oder inland water system from Gliwice to Szczecin does not constitute a uniform waterway for navigation along its entire course but, rather, consists of four distinctly different segments of the way. Each segment has its own limitations, requirements and suitability for navigation.

In summary, one can say, based on the above analysis of navigational possibilities and conditions on the Oder, that on the Gliwice Canal the navigational conditions are quite good and the depth and the width of the navigable channel do not present, at least at the present volumes of traffic, any significant problems. On the channelized Oder, even with the minimum guaranteed depth of 150 centimeters and with the 60 meter wide channel, the navigation conditions are far from satisfactory. The major obstacles to movement of barges on this portion of the way, in addition to a shallow channel, are the numerous locks with relatively small chambers of various dimensions. The middle Oder is the longest sector and the least suitable for navigation because even the minimum depth of 125 centimers in drought years cannot be maintained during the whole navigational season, thus presenting a significant problem

74

to continuous transit. The most suitable sector for navigation, with adequate depths and widths of navigable channel, is the lower Oder.

If the Oder is to be expected to play a major role in providing the service of transportation and to handle present and future barge traffic, it is imperative that the waterway attains a certain degree of uniformity, particularly in maintaining minimum depths and widths of navigable channels and size of locks. Adequate size of the waterway is considered absolutely essential.

Type of Floating Equipment and Methods of Navigation

The annual carrying capacity of the Oder River has been estimated, by the Polish planners, to be as high as ten million tons. Records show, however, that both agencies which are navigating on the Oder, Żegluga na Odrze and Żegluga Szczecinska, carried in 1970 only 3,495,168 tons, therefore, utilizing barely 35 percent of the waterway's estimated carrying capacity.[12] One of the possible reasons for the low utilization of the Oder waterway, aside from the shipper's lack of cost consciousness and the authorities' general neglect of the waterway, is the acute shortage of floating equipment. This shortage of floating equipment is not only quantitative but also qualitative. The situation from year to year is greatly improving as can be noted by the increase in absolute tonnages carried by the waterway and also by the number of operative units in service as shown in Table 3.4. Nevertheless, in comparison with other European countries, the Polish shallow draft fleet and its utilization is very meager indeed.

As one can see from the table below, quantitatively there is an assortment of floating equipment on the Oder, ranging from the most modern pusher type towboats through self-propelled high speed barges to somewhat antiquated wooden dumb barges. In recent

---

12
   From the records of the Central Statistical Office (Główny Urząd Statystyczny), Warsaw, 1971.

TABLE 3.4.

TYPE OF FLOATING EQUIPMENT OPERATING ON THE ODER

Type of Equipment	1955	1959	1964	1968	1970
Tugboat	21	21	65	45	31
Dumb Barge	278	233	210	129	80
Self-Propelled Barge	11	14	137	166	229
Towboat (Pusher)	---	---	24	48	78
Hopper (Barge)	---	---	85	138	241

Source: Data for years 1955, 1959, 1964, 1968, and 1970 obtained from the agency Żegluga na Odrze.

years, an attempt has been made to standardize and to systematically liquidate the old dumb barges and to replace them with self-propelled crafts and standardized hoppers which can be made up into flotillas.

The most pronounced changes in the type and utilization of floating equipment are indicated in Table 3.5. below. Both agencies navigating on the Oder, Żegluga na Odrze and Żegluga Szczecinska, are moving away from using the less economical dumb type barge and replacing them with self-propelled barges and various types of hoppers. In 1955, there were only eleven self-propelled barges and no flotillas navigating on the Oder, therefore, approximately 90 percent of the total tonnage carried by both agencies was carried in the dumb type barges. Since 1959, however, fleet and shore installations operating on the Oder have gone through a process of considerable modernization.

Barge size frequently reflects channel conditions, industry demands, and lock sizes. The type of barges operating on the Oder are listed in Table 3.6. For example, the three basic sizes which were most commonly used prior to 1959 on the Oder River system are: first, the two types of "Wrocław" barges, 55

76

TABLE 3.5.

MOVEMENT OF COMMODITY ON THE ODER BY TYPE
OF CRAFT USED BY ŻEGLUGA NA ODRZE

Type of Equipment	1965	1966	1968	1970
in tons				
TOTAL	2,052,390	2,527,617	2,795,041	3,133,027
Dumb Barges	1,068,941	1,057,751	710,667	454,288
Self-Propelled				
Barges	725,503	824,732	1,114,497	1,303,334
Flotillas	257,946	645,134	969,877	1,375,398
in thousand ton-kilometers				
TOTAL	1,121,187	1,367,082	1,502,225	1,655,500
Dumb Barges	523,423	586,302	328,973	254,947
Self-Propelled				
Barges	472,803	569,676	800,019	792,985
Flotillas	124,961	211,104	373,233	607,569

Sources: Główny Urząd Statystyczny, Statystyka Żeglugi Sródlądowej i Dróg Wodnych Sródlądowych, 1968, Nr. 48 (Warsaw: 1969), Table 8, p. 5.; 1970 figures obtained from the records of the agency "Żegluga na Odrze", July, 1971.

by 8 meters. The dimensions of these reflect the size and limitations of the locks in the upper sector of the channelized Oder. The second type is the 65 by 8 meters Plauer barge which was primarily employed in the lower sectors of the river. Since 1960, new types of floating equipment have appeared on the Oder, BM type motor barges and Tur and Bizon hoppers whose overall dimensions are not much different from the old equipment cited above.

Figure 3.12. graphically shows the relationship between draught and load capacity of the different types of barge operation on the Oder River system.

The process of modernization of the fleet, due to operative differences, did not affect both navigational agencies at an equal rate. By converting the data in Table 3.5. into percentages one can exemplify this point. For example, of the total tonnage carried by Żegluga na Odrze, in 1965, 52 percent was carried in dumb type barges whereas self-propelled barges and flotillas carried 35 and 13 percent, respectively. In the same year, Żegluga Szczecinska carried 81 percent of the total tonnage in the dumb

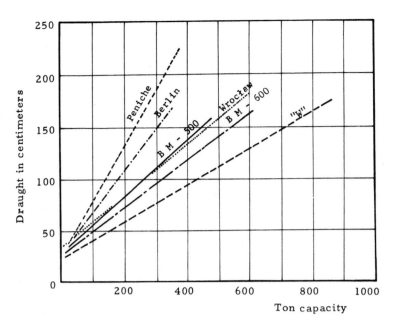

FIGURE 3.12.: DRAUGHT AND CAPACITY OF TYPICAL BARGES OPERATING ON THE ODER

type barges and only 8 percent in self-propelled and 10 percent in flotillas.[13] The operative differences and, consequently, the dissimilarity in the type of craft used by both agencies to carry commodity became more apparent in 1968 and even more so in 1970. Each type of craft listed above and operated by Żegluga na Odrze has an equal share in the movement of commodity, whereas in the Żegluga Szczecinska one detects a greater degree of specialization. Żegluga Szczecinska depends heavily on the hopper type barge which is made up into flotillas carrying over 70 percent of the total tonnage.[14] The use of dumb

[13] Główny Urząd Statystyczny, Statystyka Żeglugi Sródlądowej i Dróg Wodnych Sródlądowych 1968, Nr. 48 (Warsaw: 1969), Table 8, p. 5; 1970 data from the records of the agency Żegluga Szczecinska, August, 1971.

[14] Ibid.

TABLE 3.6.

TYPES OF BARGES NAVIGATING ON THE ODER RIVER

| Barge Type | Length (meters) | Total Length of Tow | Breadth (meters) | Draught | | Tonnage Capacity |
				Empty (meters)	Loaded (meters)	
Peniche	38.5	-----	5.0	0.26	0.24	374
Berlin	50.0	-----	6.0	0.30	1.60	335
"W"	55.0	-----	11.0	0.24	1.75	857
Wrocław	55.0	-----	8.0	0.34	1.75	536
Wrocław (Large)	55.0	-----	8.0	0.34	1.84	564
Plauer	65.0	-----	8.0	0.34	1.89	692
Oder (Finow)	55.0	-----	7.8	0.30	1.70	500
BM - 500	56.75	-----	7.5	0.30	1.70	465
BM - 600	70.72	-----	9.0	0.30	1.60	610
Hopper (BP-600)*	48.13	118.9	8.98	0.30	1.60	600
Hopper (BP-200)*	31.28	82.2	10.2	0.30	1.60	200

Note: * Tow unit on the Oder consists of pusher towboat and two barges.

Source: Records from the office of Żegluga na Odrze, Wrocław, 1968 and 1971.

type barges and self-propelled barges by this agency is at a minimum.

This dissimilar utilization of floating equipment by the two agencies arose from economic needs and both the technical and physical differences of the waterway. The small sector of the lower Oder on which the agency Żegluga Szczecinska operates is without locks and is the deepest and widest portion of the river. In addition, the type of commodity carried, large shipments and small average distance of 68 kilometers in 1970, makes hopper barges which can be assembled into integrated tows an economical and highly desirable craft. So the tendency here is to replace the antiquated dumb barges of the Pre-World War II period with a modern hopper, deck barge, car-float, and tank barge type of craft.

It is considered by authorities in the field of inland water transport that fully integrated tows are the most economic means of carrying large quantities of commodity. The fundamental advantage in using craft which can be assembled into tows is that (as shown in Figure 3.13.) a single motive power can be applied to a multi-movement unit. Particularly when the break-up of integrated tows can be held at a minimum along the way, from the point of origin to the point of destination, the economy of the cost of movement can also be held at a minimum.

In the upper portion of the Oder, where the agency Żegluga na Odrze operates, the physical and technical conditions of the routeway limit the use of integrated tows. Narrow river channels and the small radius of the channel curvature limits the size and hinders maneuverability of the large pusher flotillas. In other words, the channel dimensions have a limiting effect on the maximum number of barges that can be assembled into a tow. In addition, constant break-up of tows into small units which would permit passage through narrow locks make this type of operation on long distances with a great number of locks economically prohibitive. The integrated tow is generally efficient for the carriage of a large volume of a single commodity over a long distance on a continuing basis.

FIGURE 3.13.: PUSHER TUR WITH TWO BP-200 BARGES APPROACHING LOCK AT WROCŁAW (POPOWICE)

81

Out of the seven navigation agencies operating on Polish inland waterways, the Żegluga na Odrze has the largest number of locks and the shipments on the Oder are, on the average, the longest. The average distance of the commodity moved on the Oder in 1970, was 529 kilometers.[15] Therefore, the physical limitations of the way, long distances, relatively small shipments and type of commodity carried favors the self-propelled craft in the long distance movement where speed and flexibility is at a premium while the traditional method of pulling dumb barges by tugboat and the newly introduced method, since 1968, of push towing are primarily used on short distances.

It is generally accepted that the push-towing is a much more preferable means of movement to that of pull-towing; unfortunately, few conclusive test results have been published regarding a comparison between these two methods of navigation. Based on several experiments by Dravo Corporation, there seems to be little doubt that pull-towing, especially when practiced with a short tow-line, is less efficient than push-towing because in the former case the wake of the propeller increases the resistance of the first barge. When towed on a long line of at least 50 meters in length the barge is steered clear of the propeller wash, so that its effect is almost negligible.[16] In the case of the Oder River, due to the physical limitations of the navigable channel, the length of the towing line varies greatly in each sector.

[15]
Ibid.

[16]
Albert J. Dawson, The Development of Economic Potential of Inland Waterways Transportation (Pittsburgh: Dravo Corporation, 1956), p. 3.

Most likely the best comparison of push towing
and pull towing was obtained in experiments by
Beschoren.[17] A summary of the results obtained in the
experiments are shown below in the form of a graph.
In examination of Figure 3.14. it appears that at
least 10 percent less horsepower is needed in pushing
as compared with pulling. At higher speeds in-line
towing was appreciably better than towing of coupled
barges. The negative factors in using pull-tows, as
they may apply to navigation on the Oder, is the low
average speed of 5.1 kilometers per hour, prolonged
anchorage of tugs which can only operate in their
respective sectors, and the difficulty and complexity
in the make-up of tows.

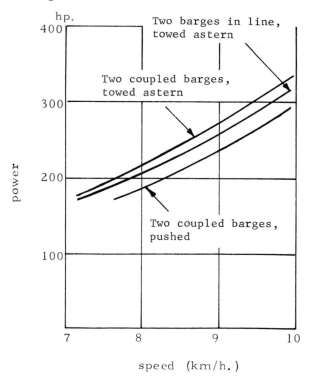

FIGURE 3.14.:   COMPARATIVE POWER REQUIREMENTS FOR VARIOUS METHODS OF
                TOWING

17
   K. Beschoren, Schieben und Ziehen in Schleppdienst, Werft Rederei und
Hafen 1931, XIII, pp. 254-259.

Movement of tugs on their respective sector is shown in Figure 3.15. It is interesting to note the difference in draft and horsepower of the tugs operating on each sector. For example, on the sector from Wrocław to Kostrzyń, the new 400 horsepower Bizon pusher is used to push only two barges as greater horsepower is required to overcome propulsive resistance in a relatively shallow channel.

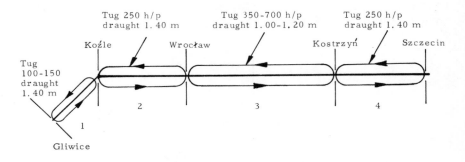

FIGURE 3.15.: MOVEMENT OF TUGS ON THE ODER BY SECTOR

Previously the author divided the Oder system into four sectors according to physical limitations and suitability of its navigable channel. However, if one looks at the navigational practice on the Oder River system, particularly in the make up of tows, one can detect additional variations within the above discussed sectors. The make up of tows on the Oder are dependent on the level of water and the number and size of locks on the individual sector of the channel. Slight variations in the level of water have a grave influence on the type of vessels that can navigate the respective sectors, tonnages, and the maximum permissible number of units in the tow. By looking at Table 3.7. one can see that there is a limitation of the navigability of the self-propel

84

TABLE 3.7.

DIMENSION OF VESSELS ON VARIOUS SEGMENTS OF THE ODER RIVER

Segment	Km. on Oder	Maximum Permissible Dimension				Minimum Water Depth	Type of Vessel
		Single Self-Propel Barges Length m	Width m	Push-Tows Length m	Width m		
From Racibórz To Koźle	51.0 95.6	41.0	5.0	-----	-----	120 Cm.	1
From Koźle To Wrocław	95.6 254.0	71.0	9.0	114.0	9.0	150 Cm.	1,2,3,4,5,6, 7,8,9,10
From Wrocław To Kostrzyń	254.0 542.4	71.0	9.0	118.0	9.0	130 Cm. 160 Cm.	1,2,3,4,5,6, 7,8,9,10,11
From Kostrzyń To Szczecin	542.4 741.6	71.0	11.0	118.0 123.0	9.0 11.0	130 Cm. 160 Cm.	1,2,3,4,5,6, 7,8,9,10,11
On Western Oder		No Limit		156.0	11.0	250 Cm.	1,2,3,4,5,6, 7,8,9,10,11
Gliwice Canal		71.0	9.0	92.0	9.0	300 Cm.	1,2,3,4,5, 6,7,8,9

Types of Vessels: 1) Penicze; 2) Berlin; 3) "W"; 4) Wrocław; 5) Wrocław-Large; 6) Plauer; 7) Oder (Finow); 8) BM-500; 9) BM-600; 10) Push tow (BP-200); 11) Push tow (BP-600).

85

barges and push-tows on various segments of the Oder system. For example, on the sector from Koźle to Wrocław, an important link between the Upper Silesian Industrial District (GOP) and the rest of the Oder River, the push-tow type BM-600 cannot operate. The sheer volume of movement on this sector, however, certainly demands large containers. The physical limitations affecting traditional methods of naviga- tion, pull-towing, on various segments on the Oder River are presented graphically. In Figure 3.16., the vertical lines divide the Oder system into four sectors and the horizontal lines indicate variable water levels during the navigation season. One can see as the water level falls the number of units in the tow also declines. Taking into consideration navigational methods, type of floating equipment, and the physical limitations of the navigable channel of various sectors within the Oder system as presented in Table 3.7. and Figure 3.16., one can derive a general description of each sector's suitability for navigation. In reviewing navigational regulations, it was not surprising to find a reflection of these phy- sical limitations within the system.[18]

For example, in the first sector, the Gliwice Canal, in order to maintain sufficient speed of move- ment, the pull-tows can be comprised of as many units as can move through the four locking operations. The width of the channel is sufficient to permit the coupling of barges, but the total length of the tow should not exceed 320 meters according to regulations. The self-propel barges cannot exceed 71.0 meters in length and 9.0 meters in width. In the case of push- tows, due to the fact that regulations forbid un- coupling of barges as they move through the locks, the tows cannot exceed 92.0 meters in length and 9.0 meters in width.

On the Oder proper from Koźle to Szczecin, there are significant differences in the composition of

[18]
  Rada Narodowa Miasta Wrocławia, Dziennik Urzędowy (Przepisy Żeglugowe) Nr. 6, (Wrocław: 23 September 1968).

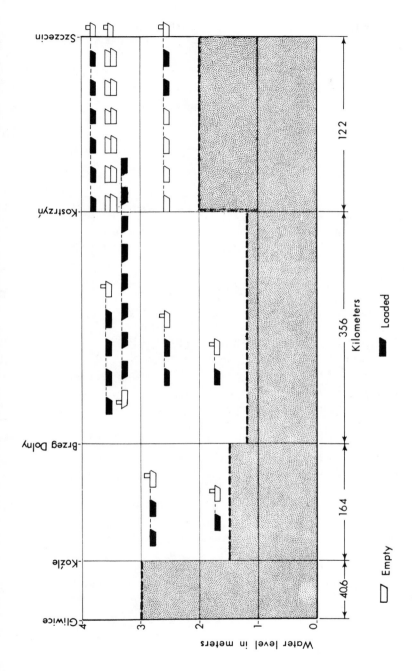

FIGURE 3.16.: TOWING METHODS ON THE INDIVIDUAL SECTORS OF THE ODER WATERWAY

87

FIGURE 3.17.: PUSHER TUR ON THE ODER

tows and methods of navigation between up and down
river movements on the individual sectors. According
to regulations, which reflect the physical characteristics of each sector of the Oder waterway, the
tows moving down the river may consist of the following units:

a) On the Upper Oder from Koźle to Brzeg Dolny,
the channelized portion of the river, during
high water the size of a tow cannot exceed
what can pass through a single locking
operation in Bartoszewice. During high and
low water level the pull tow, in movement up
the river, is limited to two units, regardless of its size. In the movement of a tow
train down the river, it may not exceed 340
meters in length during high water level.

b) On the Middle Oder, the freely flowing river,
from Brzeg Dolny to Kostrzyń, at the water
level of 2.8m, at Malczyce, a maximum tow
can consist of five units.

c) On the Lower Oder from Kostrzyń to Szczecin,
barges towed astern in line may consist of
six loaded or twelve empty, two loaded and
four empty, depending on the water level.
The number of barges in the make up of push-
tows cannot exceed six and their total maximum width cannot exceed 16.5 meters.

The tows moving up the river may consist of the
following number of units:

a) Above Brzeg Dolny, on the channelized Oder,
the limitation to the size of a tow in the
direction of Koźle is that the tow should not
have to go through more than a double locking
operation.

b) Below Brzeg Dolny, on the freely flowing
Oder, at high water level the tows can consist of eight barges but the total length of
the tow cannot exceed 460 meters. In the
movement up the river, on the deep freely
flowing segment of the Oder, loaded barges
cannot be coupled together while the empty

89

barges can be coupled together if their
total width does not exceed 16.5 meters.
Push-tow operations up the river, as in the
case of movement down the river, consists, at
maximum, of three units, a tug and two barges.

As one can see, from the description above, there are
significant differences in the movements up and down
the Oder River. In both cases, as the physical limitations become less stringent in the lowest portion
of the Oder River, the possibilities in size and make
up of the tows increase significantly. The upper
portion of the waterway presents the greatest physical
limitations.

By comparison to pulled and pushed tows, self-
propelled barges outside of tonnage limitations do
not present such a dilemma. A single unit, self-
propelled barge with an average speed of 6.8 kilometers on the Upper Oder and 9.8 in the Lower sector
executes the entire carrying operation from the point
of origin to the point of destination without major
physical constraints.[19] Therefore, where physical
and technical limitations of the channel would limit
the use of modern push flotillas, where distances
are great and speed is crucial, the motorized barges
proved to be the most versatile and efficient type
of river vessel. This is true of both domestic and
international movement.

Rate of Growth of Facilities Versus Traffic
The rebirth of traffic on the Oder River since the
conclusion of the hostilities in 1945 has been rather
spectacular in spite of the general lack of facilities.
Judging by the small investment in the inland waterways as a segment of the economy, it appears that the
Polish government sought to meets its demand for
water transport, in spite of an obvious need for an
efficient system, through greater utilization of the
existing fleet, inadequate routeway, and archaic

19
   Główny Urząd Statystyczny, Rocznik Statystyczny Transportu 1945-1966
(Warsaw: 1967), Table 40, p. 481.

shore installations. Irrespective of this limited investment in inland waterway transportation, the total freight traffic carried by Żegluga na Odrze has increased from 30 thousand tons in 1946 to 3,133 thousand tons in 1970. During this time, investment in inland waterways, in absolute terms, increased to 449.5 million złotych; but, in relative terms, in comparison with other modes of transportation, actually decreased from 1946 to less than 4 percent in 1970.[20]

In view of this deliberate government policy of putting inland waterways on short ration, it would be interesting to see how an agency navigating on the Oder with its limited fleet and inefficient shore installations coped with the ever-increasing demand for its services. This can be accomplished by examining the rate of growth of traffic on the river with the rate of growth of transport facilities. Taking the agency Żegluga na Odrze at any point in time, the distance which freight must be hauled, the speed at which barges move, and the length of time it takes to unload a barge, one obtains a degree of efficiency and the ability of the mode to satisfy the quantitative and qualitative demands for its services. The shorter the haul and the quicker the terminal operations, the more tonnage the mode can load and deliver with a given amount of equipment. This generalization is not exclusive to inland waterways but can be applicable to any mode of transportation. The more efficiently the system is operated the greater the productivity that can be obtained with less line and equipment.

In trying to estimate the existing stock of the Żegluga na Odrze, in order to make an analysis of its total carrying capacity, the author was only able to obtain a few figures from scarce Polish statistics.

20
  Ibid., Tables 24 and 25, pp. 30-32; Władysław Magiera, "Naklady Inwestycyine Na Drogi Wodne," Gospodarka Wodna, Nr. 1 (January, 1970).

These figures, nevertheless, indicate that with the resumption of navigation on the Oder in 1946, the Żegluga na Odrze had in stock 9 tugboats and 28 dumb barges with a total carrying capacity of 13,000 tons.[21] Examination of the latter data leads the author to believe that there has been a significantly greater utilization of floating equipment by Żegluga na Odrze than on the rest of the Polish waterways. For example, in 1970, the movement of empty barges by Żegluga na Odrze in relation to the total movement was only 9.8 percent; however, if one compares this with the operation by Żegluga Szczecinska, its ratio of empties to the total movement is 44.2 percent.[22] In the utilization of motive power in the same year by Żegluga na Odrze, only 5.4 percent horsepower/ kilometers was used in the movement of empty barges where in Żegluga Szczecinska as high as 23.3 percent was utilized in movement of empty barges.[23]

The addition to the carrying capacity for the years from 1946 through 1970 can be examined in Table 3.8.

If one compares the data in Table 3.8. with the data in Table 3.9. which shows the rate of growth of traffic on the Oder, one is able to make the generalization that the expansion of capital equipment of the system has been less than proportional to the increase in volume of freight handled. Instead, it appears that the Żegluga na Odrze has been under continuous pressure until 1959 from the authorities to improve their performance in attaining optimum

21
  Estimate based on personal interview with the Chief Economist of the Zjednoczenie Żeglugi, Wrocław, July, 1968.

22
  Główny Urząd Statystyczny, Statystyka Żeglugi Sródlądowej i Dróg Wodnych Sródlądowych (Warsaw: 1972), Table 67, p. 54.

23
  Ibid., Table 68, p. 55.

productivity from the old renovated facilities. In this task the agency has failed unequivocally.

To illustrate this differential rate of growth of traffic versus the transportation facilities on the Oder, the author reduced the absolute figures in Tables 3.8. and 3.9. to a common denominator, an index where 1950 traffic, barge capacity and motive power equal 100. Figure 3.18. shows the rise of the Oder's freight traffic and the rise of Żegluga na Odrze fixed capital, of which the motive power and barges are its two primary elements. A semi-logarithmic scale was used for the purpose of examining the rate of growth rather than absolute changes in tonnages and floating equipment from year to year. As is shown in the figure, the motive power and barge total capacity increased slightly from the base year of 1950 in relationship to a large increase in river freight traffic. The sharp drop in freight traffic in 1969 was a result of a prolonged drought which interrupted navigation on the Oder for 102 days.

The data presented in the two tables below has very interesting aspects. First, the rate of growth, in absolute terms, particularly since 1960 has been very sharp in keeping with the vigorous national re-development of the floating equipment of Żegluga na Odrze. The two trend lines from the two periods, 1946 to 1952, and 1960 to 1970, computed by the least squares method, shows an estimated average annual overall traffic increase at the rate of 45 and 11 percent, respectively. In the same two periods, motive power increased 36 percent in the first period and nearly 7 percent in the second period while barge capacity increased annually 45 and 10 percent. Secondly, a notable aspect of traffic development is its surprisingly good fit to the straight line trend for these two periods. The actual rate of growth in the post reconstruction period for all inland waterway traffic was 14 percent per year, thus closely approximating the estimated rate of growth. The findings below may lead one to speculate that the actual tonnages on the Oder River were predetermined by barge total ton capacity and the motive power.

TABLE 3.8.

GROWTH OF INLAND WATERWAY FLEET

Year	Motive Power Horsepower	Index 1950 = 100	Barges--Total Ton Capacity	Index 1950 = 100
1946	1,953	6	13,000	7
1947	9,706	29	64,485	33
1948	20,045	60	139,000	71
1949	30,108	91	170,963	87
1950	33,123	100	195,876	100
1951	33,123	100	236,000	120
1952	33,123	100	253,130	129
1953	33,096	100	238,000	121
1954	32,883	99	227,485	116
1955	31,887	96	220,312	112
1956	32,588	98	214,924	110
1957	33,911	102	207,803	106
1958	33,766	102	206,649	106
1959	33,291	101	210,836	108
1960	32,826	99	221,205	113
1961	32,476	98	237,352	121
1962	33,521	101	257,190	131
1963	36,521	110	284,649	145
1964	40,273	122	323,146	165
1965	44,763	135	367,550	188
1966	48,798	147	390,631	199
1967	50,358	152	409,679	209
1968	54,120	163	458,736	234
1969	55,324	167	489,267	250
1970	57,367	173	573,468	293

Source: Data obtained from the office of the agency Żegluga na Odrze, Wrocław, 1971.

94

TABLE 3.9.

GROWTH OF FREIGHT TRAFFIC ON THE ODER

Year	In 1,000 Tons	Increase From Previous Year (%)	Index 1950 = 100	In Million Ton Kilometers	Average Distance in Km.
1946	30	2	4	44.4	---
1947	125	316	16	59.2	---
1948	440	252	58	193.1	---
1949	735	69	98	284.2	---
1950	758	2	100	222.2	---
1951	946	25	125	286.1	---
1952	1,298	37	171	464.1	---
1953	1,223	-6	161	793.9	---
1954	1,634	34	216	490.4	---
1955	1,620	-1	214	643.3	---
1956	1,216	-25	160	534.0	415
1957	1,392	14	184	601.9	432
1958	1,230	-12	162	570.5	462
1959	1,399	14	184	530.7	378
1960	1,616	16	213	759.6	467
1961	1,518	-6	200	709.9	465
1962	1,626	7	214	657.4	404
1963	1,802	11	238	841.2	463
1964	1,897	5	250	1,035.6	544
1965	2,052	8	270	1,121.1	546
1966	2,528	23	334	1,367.0	542
1967	2,751	9	362	1,432.5	521
1968	2,796	2	369	1,502.2	537
1969	2,212	-21	292	958.8	433
1970	3,133	42	413	1,655.5	528

Sources: Years 1946 to 1956 from the records of Główny Urząd Statystyczny (Central Statistical Office), Warsaw; years 1957 to 1966 from Główny Urząd Statystyczny, Rocznik Statystyczny Transportu 1945-1966, Table 1 (214), p. 495; years 1967 to 1970 from the office of the agency Żegluga na Odrze, Wrocław, 1971

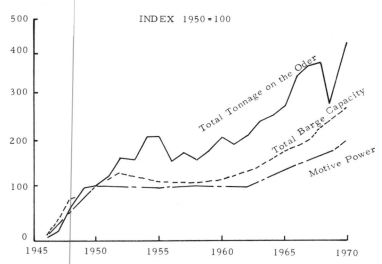

INDEX 1950 = 100

Total Tonnage on the Oder

Total Barge Capacity

Motive Power

FIGURE 3.18: GROWTH OF TRAFFIC, MOTIVE POWER, AND VEHICLE ON THE ODER
RIVER 1946-1970

Source: Based on data in Tables 3.8. and 3.9.

In the Post-World War II period from 1946 to the
present one may distinguish in the annals of the Oder
River navigation three well-marked stages.   Each
stage is a characteristic of the agency's attempt to
meet its quantitative and qualitative demand for
movement.   The first stage extends from the period
following the conclusion of the war through 1952, in
the course of which the agency Żegluga na Odrze
employed its entire energy and ingenuity in the intense reconstruction of what the military operations
had destroyed.   As was mentioned in the preceding
pages, navigation was resumed in 1946, with the
agency's entire fleet consisting of 9 tugboats and
28 barges.   All other sunk and damaged units of the
former German river fleet which lent themselves to
being repaired, 280 barges and 60 tugboats, had been
made operational in 1949 by the river shipyards.[24]
Complete reconstruction of the river installations

24
  Based on the author's personal interview with the Chief Engineer of
the river shipyards "Wrocławska Stocznia Rzeczna", July, 1968.

such as dock facilities, warehouses, locks, reservoirs, were largely completed by 1950. By that time, however, the tonnages carried by Żegluga na Odrze attained the 758,000 ton mark and 222 million ton-kilometers.[25] It soon became apparent that the agency, Żegluga na Odrze was unable to meet the rising demand for inland water transportation with its fleet. The agency's inability to cope with the rising demand for services of transportation stemmed largely from the fact that the greater part of the reconstructed fleet and shore installations were old and inefficient which, in turn, resulted in constant breakdowns. To illustrate this point, one can cite the example that the average age of a barge in the agency's inventory at that period was forty-one years old while the average age of a tug was fifty years. Up until 1959 the official policy of the planning authorities was to minimize the investment in Poland's inland waterways. The navigational agencies were instructed to do the best possible with the existing stock and equipment.

In spite of the fact that Żegluga na Odrze achieved, what some planners term, a maximum utilization of transportation facilities, serious operational problems did develop by 1954, which marks the second stage of the Polish experience in navigating the Oder. Surprisingly, in view of the crisis, no immediate steps were taken by the planning authorities to remedy this situation. An increase in inland water transportation's share of the total investment in the transportation segment of the economy was not ordered by the government until 1959. Nevertheless, before one judges the rationality of the decision of Polish planners and the seriousness of the transportation crisis in the 1954-1959 period, one should take two important points into consideration. The first is the demonstrated capacity of the agency Żegluga na Odrze to move relatively large tonnages over a long distance simply by using the antiquated facilities.

----

[25]
  See Table No. 3.9.

In that case, perhaps, only a relatively small annual increment of investment in the inland waterway sector of the economy would have averted the transport crisis which did develop. Therefore, the government's policy would have to be considered not entirely wrong. The second consideration relates to the supply of critical materials and other resources necessary for capital formation in real terms. In this connection one must also consider the question of timing. Perhaps the volume of steel which would have been necessary for the construction of floating equipment in 1952 to forestall the transportation crisis of 1954-1959 on the Oder could not have been diverted without serious consequences to a newly industrializing Polish economy.

By the end of 1958, the government by allocating additional capital to inland waterways was able to check the transportation crisis in a relatively short time. Such prompt success in mastering the crisis gives one reason to speculate that, aside from a shortage of economic resources, the crisis occurred due to general lack of interest and neglect of the inland waterway on the part of Polish planners.

The third period extends from 1959 to the present. The year 1958 is a significant year for navigation on the Oder as the decision was reached by the Council of Ministers of the Polish Peoples Republic to modernize the river's fleet, shore installations, including locks, and the navigable channel. The large concentration of industry in Upper and Lower Silesia and the difficulty and rapidly rising costs in the transporting of raw materials and other bulk commodity by rail contributed to renewed interest in the Oder River as an artery of transportation. Henceforth, in response to the optimistic forecasts that the tonnages carried by Żegluga na Odrze would rise by 1972 to 11 million tons, the government embarked on an ambitious long-range plan to expand and modernize the fleet and navigational facilities on the Oder.

One of the long-range projects involves construction and improvements in the reservoir system of the Oder River basin which would extend the navigation season. For example, in 1969, due to the low water

98

level the season lasted only 102 days as, for all practical purposes, navigation stopped on the 18th of August. As a direct consequence of deepening the navigable channel, thus maintaining a higher minimum water level, the regularity of traffic and increase in tonnage capacity of the individual barge from the present 60-75 percent of their total capacity can also be realized. These improvements in routeway together with the modernization of the fleet, transfer facilities, locks, and aids in navigation would contribute to an increase in the Oder's total transfer capacity. Unfortunately, up to the present time, outside of modernizing the fleet, very little of this grandiose plan has been accomplished and traffic on the Oder is closely approaching the technical limitations of the routeway. Substantial bottlenecks have already developed in spite of new floating equipment. The effectiveness of new floating equipment has been minimized by the fact that this equipment was constructed in view of constraining physical limitations of the navigable channel. In total, this probably has discouraged some traffic that would otherwise have moved on the river in recent years.

It is incredible that the Polish authorities do not take a greater interest in the nation's inland waterways. For example, an additional connection of the Oder with the Vistula, particularly in the south, through the Upper Silesian Industrial District (GOP) would make this river a channel of communication of considerable importance. Such a connection is desperately needed and it would demonstrate in absolute terms the Oder's direct bearing on the economic development within the area.

Chapter IV
Economics of Inland Waterways

Modern industrial experience suggests to the student
of transportation that all modes seem to evolve more
or less together as each of these modes, in the past
and at present, are intimately related to one
another in the existing transportation system.
Therefore, elimination of one mode or its total
substitution by another would necessitate
considerable alterations in the entire transportation system. Thus it seems reasonable to argue
against dramatic and total replacement of one of
the present modes of transportation by innovation.
It is readily apparent that virtually all the
modes of transportation that have ever existed are
still "alive" somewhere on the surface of the
earth. However, this does not negate the idea that,
in competition between modes, an adjustment of roles
is generally made so that all continue to exist
and develop, although at different rates. Very
seldom the newer and better method entirely sup-
plants the old but rather relegates it to a certain
limited field.
   The fact that each mode of transportation
can perform some functions very well and other
functions only moderately well does not suggest
that any single mode is unimportant, inferior,
or obsolete. The modern transportation industry
offers the shipper, depending on his needs a vast
array of services at different prices. Generally,
agencies with relatively low terminal costs and
high line-haul costs have an advantage for
shorter hauls, whereas agencies involving
high terminal pickup and delivery expenses and

100

low line-haul costs are in a position to compete more effectively for the longer hauls.[1]

When goods of high value per pound are shipped, the transfer charge constitutes a smaller relative addition to the total cost of the delivered article and such goods are said to be more "transportable," capable of bearing a higher transfer cost. The smaller the transfer cost, in relation to delivered price, the greater the disparity in elasticities in the demand for the services of transportation. In other words, the smaller the transfer cost in relation to the value of commodity, the greater is the range possibilities in transferring this commodity.

One of the major explanations of the current attraction of inland waterways as a mode of transportation is their very low cost rates compared to competitive forms of transportation. Indeed, the chief inherent advantage of barge movement is low line-haul costs for bulk commodity. One of the primary explanations of the increased productivity of the barge industry grows out of the technical improvement of the river transport equipment. The wave of technological improvements in the last decade in the barge industry and the vast physical changes in waterways have produced an inland water transportation service that has some unparalleled and unique characteristics. In this chapter, careful attention will be given to the benefits of inherent advantages that grow out of the technical aspects of inland water movement. Some attention will be given to the significance of these advantages for the general economy.

Demand Characteristics of Inland Waterways
In the analysis of demand characteristics, economic criteria must be applied to the barge industry as a

[1]
Frank H. Mossman and Newton Morton, Logistics of Distribution Systems (Boston: Allyn and Bacon, Inc., 1965), pp. 28-30.

LESLIE DIENES
Department of Geography

part of a circulation system as well as to the other modes of transportation. Invariably the investigation of the suitability of the barge industry turns to the analysis of comparative cost in relationship to the other modes within the transportation system. It is an undeniable fact that the low line-haul cost is the inherent advantage of water transportation. The combined factors of multiple units with single power unit and bouyancy of water makes possible the hauling of large volumes, thus operating cost per unit of freight is relatively low.[2] Cost, however, is not the only factor that a shipper takes into consideration in deciding on the suitability of a particular mode of transportation in relation to this need. Beyond the cost consideration, an important question is asked: Are the existing agencies rendering a present and potential service that is safe, efficient, reliable, and continuous in spite of adverse physical and weather conditions? It is generally agreed among student of transportation that in the matter of reliability, speed, and continuity of service, and flexibility, rail and, above all, motor transportation agencies hold an advantage over water.[3]

It must be pointed out that barge shipments lack many of the qualities offered by other modes of transportation, nevertheless, when it comes to moving large volumes at an extremely low cost per ton-kilometer the inland waterways have no competitors.[4] For example, in comparing line-haul rates, the American Waterways Operators, Inc., state that the cost of barge service to shippers

[2]
Ibid., p. 53

[3]
D. Philip Locklin, Economics of Transportation (5th ed.; Homewood, Illinois: Richard D. Irwin, Inc., 1960), pp. 634-646.

[4]
Ibid., pp. 719-721.

average three mills per ton-mile, where rail and truck service costs 15 and 65 mills per ton-mile, respectively.[5]

At this point, a question may be asked: What is the source of these superior economies of operation for barge service? In looking at the nature and structure of inland waterways as a mode of transportation one sees that there are several factors which determine the relatively low line-haul cost in comparison with other modes. Nevertheless, one of the prime explanations of barge operating efficiency, in addition to being a multi-movement unit to a single power unit, lies in the fluidity of water.[6] Thus the economy of inland waterway stems from relatively low propulsive resistance. Consequently, a tow within a channel requires less energy per unit of movement to propel the total movement than is true in the case of other transportation modes.

A high ratio of horsepower to net tons as compared with the ratio of horsepower to gross tons indicates that only a small percentage of the power goes to provide transportation, while the major percentage may go to overcome the propulsive resistance. For example, river transport can combine a 2400 horsepower towboat with as many as ten or more 2000 ton barges, a total of 20,000 tons of pay load.[7] The ensuing ratio is 0.14 horsepower net ton. To compare this with railroads, to pull the average freight train of 79 cars and 1430 net tons would require a 450 horsepower locomotive.[8] This is an average of 3.15 horsepower per net ton.

5
The American Waterways Operators, Inc., Big Load Afloat (Washington, D.C.: 1966), p. 2.

6
Mossman and Morton, pp. 28-29.

7
William W. Hay, An Introduction to Transportation Engineering (New York: John Wiley and Sons, Inc., 1961), p. 260.

8
Ibid., p. 259.

The degree of resistance as a result of movement which motive power must overcome depends wholly on the speed of movement. Figure 4.1. presents graphically the relationship between the degree of resistance to the speed of movement on rail, surface road, and water for one ton of commodity.

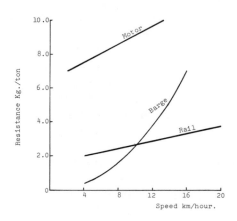

FIGURE 4.1.: RELATION BETWEEN TRACTION AND SPEED FOR VARIOUS MODES OF TRANSPORTATION

Source: Millard O. Starr, A Comparative Analysis of Resistance to Motion in Commercial Transportation (unpublished Master of Science thesis, Department of Mechanical Engineering, University of Illinois, 1945).

As one can see from Figure 4.1., with small speeds the tractive resistance on rail and road surfaces is considerably larger than on water. With an increase in speed, however, the tractive resistance on rails and roads rises slowly, approximately on diagonal straight lines, whereas the resistance on water is rising very rapidly. The skewed upward line indicates that each increment in the rise in speed the propulsive resistance on water increases disproportionately by a much higher increment. Nevertheless, with the average speed of a barge between 7-8 kilometers per hour, which is the average speed on the Oder, the propulsive resistance on water is almost half that of the rail and significantly lower than that of the highway. Thus one of the barge industry's competitive advantages stems from relatively low horsepower requirements because a major factor, in determining capacity and cost of movement, is the horsepower requirement to move one ton of pay load one kilometer. Corollary to less propulsive resistance there is significantly less vibration on water, which contributes to the low constant and operating costs of the barge industry. Consequently, capital equipment has a greater life span and requires nominal expenditures for upkeep.

The weight of the container, TARE, in relationship to the load capacity of the vehicle, in the case of inland waterways, is significantly lower in comparison with other modes of transportation.[9] For example, if one collates these relative differences in the weight of containers on various modes of transportation, one can notice that in the case of the railroad TARE ranges from 30-60 percent of the total shipment, whereas in the case of the barge industry, it ranges only from 12-20 percent of the total shipment.[10] Thus, in contrast, the dead weight of vehicles and motive power of inland waterways is of a smaller percentage to the total weight movement than is true in the case of railroad and motor transport. As a result of these differences in physical properties and requirements in containerization, the cost of vehicle and motive power per each ton of commodity is significantly smaller in the case of the barge industry than is true in the case of the other modes of transportation. To illustrate this point, one can show that to move a load of 5,000 tons by inland waterway requires a barge weighing 120 tons, in this case the TARE equals to 19.4 percent of the total shipment, while to move the same load by railroad it requires 10 cars with a total weight of 250

---

[9]
TARE is the weight of a container (vehicle) and is usually deducted from the total weight to determine the weight of the load.

[10]
The American Waterways Operators, Inc., Waterway Economics (January, 1970), pp. 77-78.

tons.[11]   The container in the case of the railroad
weighs twice as much as the container on inland
waterways.

A major economy of inland water transportation,
among other factors, results from the partially completed right of way by nature. But in many instances
the length of way, as compared to straight line distance between two points, is significantly longer on
inland waterways than is true in the case of other
modes of transportation. Relatively, the length of
way between the point of origin and the point of
destination as compared to straight line distance is
more favorable in railroads and motor transport.
Theoretically, one can approximate the railroad's
and the highway's right of ways to a straight line
where it is not always physically possible in the
case of the inland waterways. The right of ways of
inland waterways is determined by the directional
flow of the navigable river and artificial canals.
Consequently, in many instances, the movement on
inland waterways must travel longer actual distance
in kilometers to cover the same linear distance
covered by other modes of transportation. Therefore,
to compare inland waterways to other modes of transportation costs, one factor for which an allowance
must be made is the greater circuity of river routes.
While definite relationships between the length of
rail, highways, and river haul vary according to the
particular river and the particular points involved,
the comparison of distance in Table 4.1. will throw
some general light on the question.

The table shows nine points located along the
river which are also connected by rail and highway.
For the purpose of this experiment, only river locations were chosen in order for these to be accessible to all three modes of transportation. Each
mode of transportation, converging on the same points

---

[11]
  Interstate Commerce Commission, Transport Statistics in the United
States, 1965, Part I "Railroads" (Washington, D.C.: 1966), pp. 16-80.

TABLE 4.1.

RELATIVE DISTANCE BY RIVER, RAIL, AND HIGHWAY (IN KILOMETERS)

Distance		Straight Line Distance	River	R.R.	Highway	Excess Distance Over Straight Line (in %)		
From	To					River	R.R.	Highway
Gliwice	Koźle	28	41	38	40	46.4	35.7	42.9
Koźle	Opole	42	48	45	59	14.3	7.0	40.5
Opole	Gliwice	57	89	70	79	56.2	22.8	38.6
Opole	Wrocław	78	104	82	94	33.3	5.1	20.5
Brzeg	Wrocław	38	50	42	47	31.6	10.5	23.7
Wrocław	Głogów	89	183	100	152	105.6	12.4	70.8
Zielona Góra	Głogów	50	79	54	67	58.0	8.0	34.0
Wrocław	Szczecin	317	493	379	426	55.5	20.0	34.4
Szczecin	Kostrzyń	92	122	113	119	32.6	22.8	29.3

Sources: Wydawnictwo Komunikacji i Łączności, Rozkład Jazdy Pociągów PKP (Warsaw: 1969); Wydawnictwo Komunikacji i Łączności, Rozkład Jazdy Autobusów P.K.S. (Warsaw: 1969).

which are common to all three modes of transportation, has its own characteristic network or system. Here are being compared the differences expressed in percentages between river, rail, and highway transportation systems which are converging on river points, and an imaginary transportation system which contains routes connecting all these points by the shortest possible path. The shortest imaginary line between two given locations, a straight line distance, is viewed as the most desired line of movement. The amount of variation between the "desired line" of movement and actual distance, or circuity, by inland waterway, railroad, and highway is expressed in the percentages. The larger the percentage of excess distance over the straight line on the individual segments of the system, the greater is the degree of circuity and vice versa. As one can see the average circuity for the whole system varies from one system of transportation to the other. It ranges as high as 48.2 percent for inland waterway, 37.2 percent for the highway, and as low as 16 percent for railroads. Thus, in this experiment, one can say that the rail system comes the closest in comparison to approximating the ideal desired line of movement. Further, if one divides the system into smaller geographical areas, the differences on some sections between various networks are even greater. In the lower portion of the Oder River, north of Wrocław, where the river traffic is light, the excess distance on water, in comparison to the "desired line", is 62.9 percent. On the upper portion, southeast of Wrocław, where the great bulk of the Oder River traffic moves, the excess distance is significantly lower 36.4 percent.

The degree of circuity for each mode of transportation must be taken into consideration in the analysis of competitive freight rates. Therefore, it seems logical to assume that to the indicated excess of water haul distance over the railroad by 30 percent in these two portions of the Oder one should add such a share to the inland waterway transfer cost before making comparisons between these two modes of transportation. Nevertheless, the crucial issue when examining the relative benefits of river movement revolves around the relationship of river movement costs and rates compared with alternative means of transport.

One of the shortcomings of inland water movement is the low speed. The average speed on the Oder of self-propelled barges, 6.7, and tows, 5.5 kilometers per hour, cannot equal the 22 kilometers per hour of a freight train.[12] However, the time consumed between pick up of barges and receipt at the destination is less unfavorable than the actual operating speed of movement on the water implies. Barge operation is usually relatively simple and little time is consumed in making up tows and dropping them at the point of destination. Undeniably, the technical speed of a barge which can be defined as an average speed between two points of terminus is significantly smaller than the speed of vehicles in the case of other modes of transportation. However, to increase the technical speed of the tows on inland waterways would rapidly increase tractive resistance, which in turn would necessitate tugboats with higher horsepower to overcome this resistance.

The comparison of the profitability of movement by various modes of transportation does not entirely depend on their technical speed but, rather, on the total transfer time.[13] The transfer time includes, in addition to technical speed of movement, terminal time and various interruptions in movement. It is the total time that is required for a commodity to move from the point of origin to the point of destination. It is a relationship between the linear distance of movement to the total time that is required

---

12
  Główny Urząd Statystyczny, Statystyka Żeglugi Śródlądowej i Dróg Wodnych Śródlądowych 1968, Nr. 48 (Warsaw: 1969), Table 35, pp. 57-58; Główny Urzad Statystyczny, Statystyka Transportu Kolejowego 1967, Nr. 25 (Warsaw: 1968), Table 24, p. 18.

13
  Lucjan Hofman, Ekonomika Branżowa Jako Nauka: Na Przykładzie Ekonomiki Transportu (Sopot: Wyższa Szkoła Ekonomiczna, 1962), pp. 23-40.

for movement to overcome that distance. In each mode of transportation this relationship would differ because of its inherited characteristics and practices in terminus and its technical speed. The investigation of the inland waters could lead one to speculate that perhaps the difference of average transfer speed between railroad and inland waterways is not as great as the differences in their technical speed would indicate. The final criterion as to the suitability of a particular mode of transportation, in many situations, is the quantity of freight that can be moved per hour or per day between two points by a given combination of plant and equipment.

The primary prerequisite for utilizing the efficiencies of barge shipment is consolidation of the massive volume of freight at one point. This is a shortcoming to some extent. It means that many types of commodity that are not subject to such massive concentration at one point and at one time are not likely to be shipped by barge. For example, the agency Żegluga na Odrze has minimum tenders ranging between 100 to 305 tons.[14] The Polish railroad (PKP) has railroad rates for a minimum of 5 to 10 tons.[15] The requirement of such high minimum tender certainly restricts barge service to a fairly limited range of commodities.

In summary, inland water transport offers many technological advantages such as high productivity in net ton-kilometers per tugboat hour, high cargo weight to dead weight, and low horsepower per ton ratios. The disadvantages of inland water transport fall into three major categories; lack of route flexibility, slow speed, and interruption of service due to adverse weather conditions. Both the requirements and disadvantages have limited the barge industry to low grade freight for which speed is less important than quantity movement.

[14]
See Table 3.6.

[15]
Główny Urząd Statystyczny, Statystyka Transportu Kolejowego (Warsaw: 1967), p. 42.

Inland Waterways as a Part of the Circulation System

Industrial development in modern Poland could not
have been obtained without a relatively sophisticated
network of transportation and communication. Physically, Poland is well adapted to the formation of
such a network. The present pattern and densities of
transportation network in that country, however, reflect the political and administrative past of this
area. Before the end of the eighteenth century
Poland as a nation state had ceased to exist. In
three successive exploits between 1772 and 1795 it
was partitioned among its neighbors, Austria, Prussia,
and Russia, and did not emerge as a sovereign and
independent state until 1918.[16] Consequently, the
densities and patterns of railways and roads and the
location and spacing of settlements along the navigable rivers reflect the level of the economic development and the particular requirements of the three
partitioners of Poland.

Taking into consideration the whole experience
of industrialization of the area which is now Poland,
one can characterize three distinct periods. In the
first period, from 1850 to 1913, a span of sixty-three
years when no significant territorial changes took
place, each partitioner developed its subjugated area
according to its economic needs. For example, Polish
territory under the Prussian administration became the
most industrialized of all three, as a result it
attained the greatest railway densities. Unfortunately
for Polish economic needs, all the important lines
converged on the Prussian political capital, Berlin.
In comparison, the lowest density of railroad lines,
reflecting the level of economic development, was
under Russian rule. Only a few main lines converged
on Warsaw which at that time was an important manufacturing center of Tsarist Russia. As a result of

---

16
 William Langer (ed.), Western Civilization: The Struggle for Empire
to Europe in the Modern World (New York: Harper and Row, Publishers,
Inc., 1968), p. 230.

these differences in the level and the intensity of industrialization, Poland, with independence after 1918, did not inherit a fully integrated and unified transportation system suitable to its new economic needs but, rather, inherited three parts of a transportation system distinctly and drastically different from one another.

In the second period, the interwar period, Poland's energy, among other things, was absorbed not only in bringing about economic development in a predominantly agrarian economy but also in integrating segments of various transportation networks into a unified system. The aggravated need for east-west connections, such as those between Central Poland and Silesia, and Central Poland with the coast, was partially solved by construction of several main lines in the 1920's.[17]

The third period began when Poland embarked on the ambitious plan of rapid super-industrialization after 1945. The same transportation problem, however on a smaller scale, reappeared in the Post-World War II period. As the outcome of the shifting of the state's boundaries by 135 kilometers to the west, Poland acquired a portion of German territory whose transportation network was not oriented to the economic needs of Poland.

The early nineteenth century industrial experience of the area cannot be dismissed as trivial and no longer applicable and valid in the twentieth century because it created the pattern which, in many instances, acts and persists as inertia to this day. The sheer fact that there were differences in the nature, rate and intensity of economic development between the three partitioners of Poland, the differences in the direction, pattern, and density of railroad network developed, created relic patterns

17
  Teofil Lijewski, "Niektóre Problemy Badawcze w Geografii Transportu Kolejowego," Zeszyty Naukowe Szkoły Głównej Planowania i Statystyki, No. 63 (1967), p. 23.

which are still visible and operative in present day
Poland. For example, the average density of railroad
lines is 8.6 per 100 square kilometers for the entire
country.[18] However, if one takes individual województwo
into consideration, the density varies from 4.6 kilometers in województwo Lublin, formerly a part of the
Tsarist empire to as high as 18.2 kilometers in
województwo Katowice, formerly a part of Prussia.[19]
The density of surface roads also decreases from west
to east. The highest densities, as in the case of
the railroads, are in the southwestern województwa,
Katowice and Wrocław.

Different demands, both quantitative and qualitative, for the services of transportation are
supplied by different modes. However, the relative
share that each mode occupies in the total supply of
transportation varies from one economic system to the
other. The share that each mode occupies will tend
to reflect demands imposed by the economic system.
Therefore, it is necessary to look at the relative
position of each mode and compare them in terms of
a common denominator, percentages, of tons moved and
ton-kilometers by each mode of transportation.

It should be recognized that the measurement in
terms of tons carried by each mode of transportation
will give emphasis to heavy goods, where ton-kilometers
measurement will accentuate heavy commodity moved
over long distances. As one can see in Table 4.2.
and Figure 4.2., which is the graphic representation
of the table, it is possible to find various measure-
ments of the relative share of transportation with
various emphasis.

As the statistics show, the dominant mode of
transportation in the intercity movement of commodity
when measured in terms of ton-kilometers is the railroad. In 1970 it carried 81.6 percent of the total

18
  Główny Urząd Statystyczny, Rocznik Statystyczny 1968 (Warsaw: 1969),
Table 2, p. 296.

19
  Ibid.

TABLE 4.2.

INTERCITY MOVEMENT OF GOODS AND PEOPLE BY
MODES OF TRANSPORTATION, 1970
(IN PERCENTAGES OF TOTAL)

Mode	Freight Traffic		Passenger Traffic	
	% of Total Tonnages	% of Ton-Km.	% of Pass.	% of Pass.-Km.
Railroad	31.3	81.6	44.8	56.8
Motor Transport	66.8	11.7	54.8	42.2
Horse Transportation*	0.3	..	..	..
Inland Waterways	0.5	1.2	0.4	0.2
Air Transport	..	..	0.03	0.8
Pipelines	1.1	5.5	..	..

* Excluding agriculture
.. Insignificant

Source: Based on statistics in Główny Urząd Statystyczny, <u>Rocznik Statystyczny 1971</u>
         (Warsaw: 1971), Tables 6 and 7, pp. 352-353.

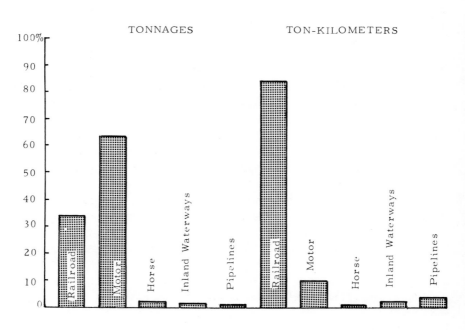

FIGURE 4.2.: RELATIVE SHARES OF THE SUPPLY OF TRANSPORTATION IN 1970

interurban traffic measured in ton-kilometers.
The only major suppliers of the service of transportation in Poland, of significantly lesser
prominence when measured in terms of ton-kilometers,
are the motor carriers. In 1970, motor transport
carried 11.7 percent of the total freight traffic
measured in terms of ton-kilometers.

However, when one looks at the percentage
share of each mode of transportation in the movement of total tonnage of intercity freight traffic,
the railroad is not the chief supplier of transportation but, rather, motor carriers. For
example, in 1970 railroads moved only 31.3 percent
of the total tonnages of freight, whereas motor
transport moved 66.8 percent. These differences of
emphasis in measurement are clearly shown in
Figure 4.2. above.

The noticeable differences between absolute
tonnages and ton-kilometers as a measurement of
a mode's relative share to the total supply of
transportation does not indicate that there is a
division of labor based on distance, but rather,
the railroad with its antiquated equipment is
moving few bulky commodities over long distances.
Concentration of industry within a small geographical area, the compactness of the country, and
the short distances between origins and destinations
favor motor carriers. Strictly from economic
considerations, motor carriers have been able to
cut into the railroad market over a broad spectrum
of commodity in short, intermediate, and long distances by offering the shipper better service.
This is true despite the fact that cost of transporting all commodities more than a short distance
by truck exceeds the cost of transporting them by
rail. As a result, motor transportation shows a
greater rate of growth in tonnages and ton-kilometers
of intercity freight service while the railroad
shows stagnation as the volume of traffic is
exceeding their maximum volume carrying capacities.
For example, the motor carrier tonnages have
increased from 110.0 million tons in 1950 to 862.6

million in 1970, an increase of 784 percent while
railroads in the same period increased only 235.6
percent.[20] It should be noted that these relative
shares have not been constant over a period of time.
Previously, the railroad was almost exclusively the
only mode of transportation in Poland. As late as
1950, railroads carried 92.2 percent of the total
intercity freight traffic.[21] While at the present
time, all modes carry more tonnages than were carried in the early Post-World War II period, the
relative share of each mode has significantly changed.
Much of the increase in tonnage in the last nineteen
years has gone to the newer and more efficient modes
of transportation, particularly to trucks and pipe-
lines.

Statistically, inland waterways in Poland have
a small share of the total transportation market
measured in either total tonnages or in ton-
kilometers. Table 4.3. shows that inland waterway
carriers had 0.3 percent of the total freight market
in 1946 and 1.2 percent in all intercity freight in
1970. The trend lines in Figure 4.3., however,
indicate that total ton-kilometers of motor and
domestic waterway freight have risen at a much
greater rate than that of the railroad.

A comparison of the percent increase in barge
traffic since 1946, with the rates of increase for
other transportation modes shown in Table 4.3.,
reveals that freight traffic on inland waterways,
in spite of the low relative position in total tonnages commodity moved, has risen very rapidly.
This rise is second only to the spectacular increase

20
  Główny Urząd Statystyczny, Rocznik Statystyczny 1970 (Warsaw: 1970),
Table 6, p. 299.

21
  Ibid.

TABLE 4.3.

INTERCITY FREIGHT MOVEMENT BY MODES (FOR SELECTED YEARS)

Mode	1946	1950	1955	1960	1964	1968	1970
	In Million Ton-Kilometers						
Rail	19,473	35,139	51,969	66,547	79,060	92,636	99,261
Truck	40	210	3,965	5,692	7,772	12,001	15,760
Pipeline	----	----	----	----	1,706	5,898	6,978
Inland Water	53	265	775	904	1,248	2,020	2,294
Air	----	1	2	3	6	12	17
TOTAL	35,566	35,615	56,834	73,187	89,187	112,567	124,310
	Percentage Distribution (of Ton-Kilometers)						
Rail	99.5	98.6	91.4	90.9	88.0	81.6	79.8
Truck	0.2	0.5	6.9	7.7	8.7	11.7	12.7
Pipeline	--	--	--	--	1.9	5.5	5.6
Inland Water	0.3	0.7	1.3	1.2	1.4	1.2	1.8
Air	*	*	*	*	*	*	.01
TOTAL	100.0	100.0	100.0	100.0	100.0	100.0	100.0
	Relative Growth						
Index 1950 100							
Rail	55	100	148	186	225	264	282
Truck	19	100	1,888	2,710	3,701	5,718	7,505
Pipeline	----	----	----	----	----	----	----
Inland Water	20	100	292	341	471	762	866
Air	----	100	200	300	600	1,200	1,700
TOTAL	99	100	160	205	252	327	349

*Insignificant

Sources: Główny Urząd Statystyczny, Rocznik Statystyczny Transportu 1945-1966 (Warsaw: 1967); Główny Urząd Statystyczny, Rocznik Statystyczny 1971 (Warsaw: 1971), p. 352.

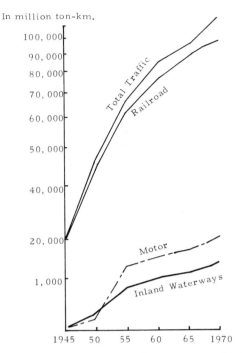

In million ton-km.

FIGURE 4.3.: THE TREND IN INTERCITY FREIGHT MOVEMENT BY MODES

Source: Based on data in Table 4.3.

in the trucking industry.[22] Particularly, since 1960, inland waterways have experienced accelerated growth in traffic.

All inland water agencies navigating Polish rivers in 1970 carried approximately 6.6 million tons, which constitutes only 0.6 percent of the total tonnages carried by the nation's transportation system.[23] The low participation of inland

---

22
Growth of air traffic has been excluded in this comparison due to the fact that it still remains relatively unimportant in the modal split measured in tons or ton-kilometers.

23
Główny Urząd Statystyczny, Statystyka Żeglugi Śródlądowej i Dróg Wodnych Śródlądowych 1970 (Warsaw: 1971), Table 1, p. 1.

118

waterways in carrying the nation's freight traffic is largely due to insufficient technological improvements on the rivers, rate structure, the lack of cost consciousness on the part of the shippers, and partially due to inherited characteristics of the mode. The most important navigable rivers in Poland are the Oder and the Vistula. In spite of a great estimated potential by the proponents of inland water transportation, the present contribution of these rivers to the total movement of commodity is rather minimal. One set of problems, among a multiplicity of others, are the technical ones. These can be divided further into two subcategories. One necessitating improvements in the existing navigable channels and the second subcategory of technical problems stem from the changes in the direction of commodity flow. The fact is that most of the rivers in Poland are not channelized or regulated. Channelization would allow a greater flexibility in the type of equipment used and the method of navigation. As a result of the Post-World War II increase in the demand for east-west commodity movement, there is an insufficient amount of east-west artificial connections to facilitate the demand. Construction of several east-west canals between the northerly flowing Oder and Vistula would link these rivers into a greatly needed unified network of inland waterways.

If one looks at the present pattern of inland waterways in Poland, it shows that two major streams, the Vistula and the Oder, are connected togther in their lower reaches, in the northern portion of the country, via the Warta and Noteć Rivers and the Bydgoszcz Canal. The northern portions of województwa Zielona Góra, Poznań, and Bydgoszcz, through which the Warta and the Noteć flow are an area of relatively low manufacturing concentration, thus such a connectivity has small economic significance. Unfortunately, no connection exists between these two rivers in the middle of the country, for example, linking Wrocław and Łódz with Warsaw which is an area of high manufacturing concentration. In the southwest, the Upper Silesian industrial district in województwo Katowice, is linked with the Oder via the Gliwice

Canal. Here, the canal serves only the function of a feeder line. Equally, there is a lack of water connection between the Upper Silesian Industrial District and the Vistula, flowing only a few kilometers to the east. As its stands now these two major rivers constitute two distinctly separate inland water systems, only casually connected in the area where there is the least need for such connectivity. Here it should be pointed out that the efficiency of the system is not judged on the merit of its individual links but on the entire network of the system connecting all focal points between desirable areas of origins and destinations.

In comparison with other navigable streams in Poland, the most important river for navigation, both from the physical and economical point of view, is the Oder. Its primary importance stems from its geographical location. Together with the Gliwice Canal, the Oder links the coal basin and heavy industry of Upper Silesia with the maritime port of Szczecin. The economic prominence of the Oder in comparison to the other Polish navigable streams can be shown by examining the total tonnages carried by inland waterways for 1970. For example, the total tonnages carried by inland waterways in Poland in 1960 was 6.8 million tons, an average distance of 308 kilometers, of which the agency Żegluga na Odrze carried approximately 46 percent at an average distance of 528 kilometers.[24] The true nature and the economic importance of the Oder River can be shown, in respect to other navigable streams, by pointing out that in terms of tonkilometers the Żegluga na Odrze carried approximately 74 percent of the entire Polish waterborne traffic.[25] The fact is that where other navigable streams in Poland and the agencies navigating on these waterways have only local significance, carrying primarily sand

[24]
From the records of Żegluga Na Odrze, Wrocław, July, 1971.

[25]
Ibid.

and gravel over short distances, the Oder River, in relative terms, is, in the true sense of the word, an important artery of transportation of both inter-regional and international level. For example, the average distance for the two local agencies navigating on the Vistula, Żegluga Warszawska and Krakowska, in 1970 was 70 and 41 kilometers respectively, while the average distance of the Żegluga na Odrze in the same year was 528 kilometers.

Administrative Structure of Poland's Transportation

Since the end of the war there have been successive administrative reorganizations of the transportation services in Poland. The reasons for these modifications have been the necessity to bring transportation into line with new administrative policies, the Soviet operational patterns of commodity flow, and above all, due to growing operational difficulties arising from rapid industrialization and urbanization.

In the People's Republic of Poland, all forms of public transportation are state owned. State ownership cannot be attributed as a peculiar characteristic of the socialist form of government but, rather, is in many respects an extension of a practice which existed before World War II in so-called capitalistic Poland. Prior to World War II, there were important state-owned transportation undertakings such as the Polish State Railways (PKP), Polish Airlines (LOT), three steamship companies, and the port of Gdynia. The first two came under the jurisdiction of the Ministry of Industry and Commerce. There was only one major railroad line, Gdynia-Silesia (completed in 1926), privately owned with a large share of foreign invest-ment, primarily French. Highway transportation, con-sisting largely of horse drawn wagons was mainly in private hands but operating licenses were issued by the somewhat obscure and insignificant Ministry of Transport. Under the jurisdiction of the Ministry of Transport were also included inland waterways, although the barges and shipping companies were privately operated. Since the railroads handled the bulk of freight and passenger traffic, it can be said that the transportation service in Poland before the war was provided by the state.

In Post-World War II Poland, once again, the state assumed the control over the modes and service of transportation. The Ministry of Transport, elevated to a new role, took over the top management of all forms of transportation with the exception of the maritime ports and the merchant marine which fell under the jurisdiction of the newly created Ministry of Shipping. In addition to the prewar state-owned transportation enterprises, several new agencies under the jurisdiction of the Ministry of Transport were created. Among these agencies were the State Highway Transportation, the State Agency for Navigation on the Vistula, and the State Agency for Navigation of the Oder.

This organizational structure of Polish transportation lasted until 1951, when the Ministry of Transport was abolished. As the problems of physical distribution became more complex in the early 1950's, the Polish planners attempted to solve the mounting and complex problems, arising from rapid economic changes, by administrative reorganizations. The highly centralized control and wide jurisdiction over the system of transportation enjoyed by the Ministry of Transportation was divided between the four newly created ministries. The former functions of the Ministry of Transport pertaining to the construction, maintenance, and operations on inland waterways and river shipyards were taken over by the newly created Ministry of Navigation.

The Ministry of Shipping was given the added responsibility of developing and coordinating a balanced transportation system. Its primary function is to move goods and people through a system of transportation. In the assignment of individual tasks to the modes and the problem pertaining to movement, the Ministry of Shipping has undisputed jurisdiction and control over the transportation modes, while the respective ministries have administrative responsibilities and technical power over their modes of transportation. In planning and coordinating further development of Poland's transportation system the Ministry of Shipping equally plays a key role. Its function here is not only to keep and provide statistical data pertaining to movement on which projected plans are based but also to coordinate and develop a balanced and uniform transportation system according to the economic, political, and social needs and objectives of the country.

The state power pertaining to inland waterways is vested in two ministries (see Figure 4.4.), the Ministry of Navigation (Ministerstwo Żeglugi) and the Ministry of Inland Waterways (Ministerstwo Dróg Wodnych). Immediately below the Ministry of Navigation (Ministerstwo Żeglugi) on the hierarchical scale, the all powerful, Association of Navigation (Zjednoczenie Żeglugi) coordinates the activities between Żegluga na Odrze, the Inland Water Shipyards (Stocznie Rzeczne) and the Inspectorate of Inland Waterways (Inspectorat Dróg Sródladowych).

The Ministry of Inland Waterways (Ministerstwo Dróg Wodnych) has several subordinate units. The most interesting one and the most important from the point of navigation is the District Directorate of Inland Waterways (Okregowy Zarzad Wodny). The entire country is divided into five districts, headed by the Directorates, with seats in Wrocław, Kraków, Warsaw, Gdańsk, and Poznań. The power and responsibilities of the District Directorate of Inland Waterways (Okregowy Zarzad Wodny) extends to one main task which is the construction and development of navigable inland waterways; this includes regulation, channelization, construction of retention reservoirs, dams and locks.

The district directorates of inland waterways (Okregowy Zarzad Wodny) are not engaged in actual construction themselves but, rather, they delegate this function to a subordinate body, the office of Water Management (Zarzad Wodny). The actual number of Water Managements under the supervision of the District Directorate depends on the size of the district and the specific characteristics of the sectors of inland waterways

123

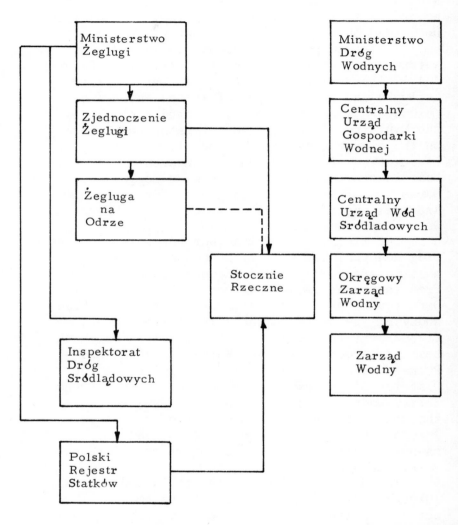

FIGURE 4.4.:   ORGANIZATIONAL STRUCTURE OF POLAND'S INLAND WATERWAYS

within the jurisdiction of a particular directorate. The actual number of Water Management offices in the district, however, may vary between four and ten.[26]

Commercial inland water ports and their facilities are under the direct jurisdiction and supervision of a given navigational agency. For example, Żegluga na Odrze has complete control over ports and facilities within the range of its operations. Other anchorages and winter quarters are under the jurisdiction and are the responsibility of the Central Office of Water Management (Centralny Urzad Gospodarki Wodnej).

Previous regulations governing movement of goods and people on inland waterways in the post-war planned economic system had to be drastically modified to meet the new economic and political conditions. Many of these laws and regulations of the interwar period were remnants of the old common laws and accepted practices differing from stream to stream, some dating from the middle ages. The postwar economic and political changes gave a splendid opportunity to break with historical inertia and to adopt codified uniform laws and regulations governing navigation on all Polish inland waterways.

The first set of such laws and regulations pertaining to movement on Poland's waterways was adopted on March 7, 1950.[27] The basis for the economic organization of inland water transportation is embedded in Article Eleven which states that commercial navigation on the nation's inland

[26] Based on the author's personal interview with the engineer at Water Management Office in Koźle, May, 1968.

[27] Prezydjum Rady Narodowej, Regulamin Nawigacyiny Na Drogach Wodnych Sródlądowych Rzeczpospolitej Polski (Warsaw: 1950).

waterways may be performed by the government's own concerns or concessionary enterprises.[28] There are nine additional articles which cover all phases of movement and related fields pertaining to inland water navigation. These laws, which are subject to periodical scrutiny and revision, were adopted by decree of the Ministry of Navigation with the collaboration of the State Economic Planning Commission, Tresury, Public Administration, Internal Security, and the Ministry of Internal Trade. Since the 1950 decree the Ministry of Navigation periodically updates the existing regulations and institutes new ones.

In accordance with the regulations, enterprises navigating on Polish inland waterways must publish rates for the shipment of goods and people which are subject to approval by the Ministry. It is interesting to note that these rates are constructed on the premise that the inland water transport or combination rail-water transport should be cheaper than railroads or motor transport. In other words, at least theoretically, the barge industry, based on rate structure, has a price advantage over other modes of transportation by administrative decree. Therefore, if one disregards the level of service differential and if one assumes that the Polish bulk commodity shipper is cost conscious, then he should be using the inland waterways wherever it is accessible.

[28] Ibid.

Chapter V

Type of Movement and Traffic Density

It is assumed in this study that the decision makers in the long run in a socialist economic system such as Poland, as in a free economy, strive to minimize the total cost of bringing goods and services to the consumer at the market place. Transportation cost is a part of the total cost of the goods offered at the market place. Therefore, the objective of the planners should be to minimize, among other costs, the cost of procuring raw materials on the side of production and the distribution cost on the side of consumption.

Theoretically, it can be stated that each mode of transportation, due to its inherent characteristics in motive power, vehicle, and way (which are the main basis for cost differences), possesses an absolute or competitive advantage in moving certain types of commodity over a certain distance. These cost differences, in offering the service of transportation, determine the place a given mode of transportation occupies in the market allocation of distribution facilities. In reality, however, due to many constraints in the competition between modes in providing the service of transportation, one can find all modes competing for various commodities at various distances.

In the preceding chapter, it was recognized that the inland water carriers, due to their inherent technological characteristics and resulting economy of scale, are best suited for bulk commodity movement. While the inland waterway carriers' high terminal pick up and delivery expenses make the mode an ineffective competitor in the short-distance hauls,

127

its low line-haul costs give the mode a competitive advantage in the longer haul. In an industrial society there is a whole array of demands, both quantitative and qualitative, for the service of transportation. Therefore, under competitive market conditions and without regulatory constraints and subsidies, modes within such a transportation system would tend to specialize, exploiting their peculiar competitive advantages.

One must remember that in a socialist economy the price system as a mechanism, as understood in capitalistic economic terms, does not exist. Therefore, it cannot be used as a measure of economic efficiency and for the purpose of resource allocation, including price differential, between modes based on its marginal or fully operative costs. The existing modal-split rather reflects rate structure derived by purely administrative decisions. This does not mean that the shipper is entirely indifferent to prices and that he lacks the desire to minimize the total transfer cost while maximizing the utility. What it really means is that the existing rate structure has very little or nothing at all to do with the inherent competitive advantage of each mode.

In this chapter, an analysis will be made of the quantitative and qualitative demands for movement on the Oder River. The primary question will be asked: What are the identifiable characteristics of the present flows? This analysis will include the type of commodity moved of both domestic and international shipments, the rate of movement, and the direction of flow on the individual segment within the Oder River network.

Quantitative and Qualitative Demand for Movement on the Oder

When considering the relative importance of the Oder River in the inland waterways of Poland, its total aggregate demand for movement should be compared with other systems in terms of the quantitative and qualitative demands. By simply looking at the supply and the demand function of inland waterways, it can be shown that in 1970 barges carried 7,915,790 tons of commodity which barely represents 0.6 percent of the nation's intercity freight traffic.[1] The state agency of Żegluga na Odrze, the principal barge company providing the service of transportation on the Oder north of Szczecin, carried 42.1 percent of the total traffic. None of the remaining six agencies operating on Polish inland waterways, as can be seen in Table 5.1. approached this sizable figure. The rate of growth expressed in the annual absolute increase in tonnages and ton-kilometers carried by Żegluga na Odrze from 1946 through 1970 is shown in Table 3.9.

Table 5.1. shows that the barge company, Żegluga na Odrze, in 1970 carried 74.3 percent of the total traffic measured in ton-kilometers. The next highest water carrier measured in ton-kilometers was Żegluga Bydgoska with 14.5 percent of the total traffic carried on Polish inland waterways. If one compares the average distances of commodities carried by each agency, it becomes apparent that unlike the rest of the Polish water carriers, who have primarily a local significance, the agency, Żegluga na Odrze, in addition to its local importance, is a carrier of national and international scope.

The analysis of qualitative demand reveals the great importance of the Oder in the movement of bulk commodities. Table 5.2. which shows the freight traffic on Poland's inland waterways by type of commodity moved, indicates that more than half of the inland waterway's national tonnage consists of sand and gravel. This, however, is not true in the case of the Oder River. Unlike the national make-up of cargo, the single most important commodity carried by the agency Żegluga na Odrze is coal, 50.8 percent of its total tonnage, whereas sand and gravel constitutes only 20.5 percent of its total tonnage. Probably, due to the geographic location of the Oder River, linking the Upper and Lower Silesian coal mines

---

[1]
From the records of Zjednoczenie Żeglugi, Wrocław, July, 1971.

TABLE 5.1.

TRAFFIC CARRIED BY INLAND WATERWAY SHIPPERS ACCORDING TO AGENCY

	In Percentages Tons			In Percentages Ton-Kilometers			Average Distance (in Km.) (1968)
	1965	1968	1970	1965	1968	1970	
Żegluga na Odrze	43.8	42.3	42.1	79.5	77.6	74.3	529
Żegluga Szczecinska	13.0	12.6	14.7	2.4	2.6	3.7	77
Żegluga Gdańska	4.2	4.0	3.8	1.0	1.0	0.9	74
Żegluga Mazurska	2.8	2.6	2.1	0.2	0.2	0.1	17
Żegluga Bydgoska	9.5	9.4	10.0	12.8	13.7	14.5	445
Żegluga Warszawska	18.5	20.9	18.6	3.3	3.9	5.1	84
Żegluga Krakowska	8.2	8.2	8.2	0.8	1.0	1.4	52

Sources: Years 1965 and 1968, Główny Urząd Statystyczny, Statystyka Żeglugi Śródlądowej i Dróg Wodnych Śródlądowych, Nr. 48 (Warsaw: 1969), Table 8, p. 5; Year 1970 from the Central Statistical Office, Warsaw, June, 1971.

with the maritime port of Szczecin, 95.1 percent of all coal carried on Polish waterways is carried by the agency Żegluga na Odrze.

The relative importance and magnitude of movement on the Oder River can be appreciated by closer examination of Table 5.2. which also indicates the Oder's share in relation to the total inland waterway movement. For example, of the fourteen types of commodities listed in Table 5.2., seven of these the agency Żegluga na Odrze carries at least 50 percent of the total tonnage. If one lists the commodities in the range between 25 percent and above of the national tonnages carried, this agency would have an impressive list of ten commodities to its credit of the fourteen listed in the table below. Even more impressive is the role of the Oder River in the inland water movement if one takes each individual commodity and the tonnages for consideration. For example, over a million and a half tons of coal, 95 percent of the total inland water coal tonnage is carried by Żegluga na Odrze. In addition, 50 percent of the ores, the entire tonnage of lignite, coke, and fertilizer, 83 percent of cement, and 44.4 percent of petroleum is carried on the Oder.

In comparing various inland waterway carriers, it can be seen that there is a greater concentration of large tonnage in fewer commodities on the Oder than is true in the case of any other inland water carrier. For example, four types of commodities carried by Żegluga na Odrze, bituminous coal, sand and gravel, ore, and fertilizer composed 97.3 percent of the agency's entire tonnage in 1970. To compare this with Żegluga Bydgoska, the agency navigating on the rivers, Noteć, Warta, and the lower portion of the Oder, outside of sand and gravel which in 1970 constituted 48.4 percent of the agency's total tonnage, there is a complete lack of commodity concentration. [2] The next highest group of commodity which

---

[2]
Główny Urząd Statystyczny, Statystyka Żeglugi Śródlądowej i Dróg Wodnych Śródlądowych 1970 (Warsaw: 1971).

TABLE 5.2.

1970 FREIGHT TRAFFIC ON INLAND WATERWAYS BY TYPE OF COMMODITY

By Type of Commodity	Carried by all Polish Water Carriers		Carried on the Oder			
	Tons	% of Total	Tons	% of Total	% of Nat. Tonnages Carried by Oder	Average Distance
Bituminous Coal	1,665,379	21.0	1,582,943	50.8	95.1	652
Lignite and Coke	26,727	0.3	26,727	0.9	100.0	624
Ore	481,084	6.1	240,484	7.7	50.0	602
Stone	426,472	5.4	36,654	1.2	8.5	543
Sand and Gravel	4,351,852	55.0	639,280	20.5	14.7	49
Petroleum	5,627	0.07	2,501	0.08	44.4	---
Metals and Metal Products	43,805	0.6	32,503	1.0	74.2	617
Cement	15,556	0.2	12,905	0.4	83.0	911
Fertilizer	384,230	4.9	384,230	12.3	100.0	453
Misc. Chemicals	31,608	0.4	8,311	0.3	26.1	414
Grain	108,797	1.4	71,391	2.3	65.6	250
Misc. Agricultural Products	81,414	1.0	29,523	0.9	36.3	341
Wood and Wood Products	212,744	2.7	26,141	0.8	12.2	98
Other Commodities	79,536	1.0	19,405	0.6	24.4	364
TOTAL	7,915,790	100.0	3,113,000			

Source: Główny Urząd Statystyczny, Przewozy Ładunków Żeglugą Śródlądową Pomiędzy Województwami i Wojewódzkie Bilanse Przewozów Ładunków 1966-1970, Nr. 92 (Warsaw: July, 1971).

was 8.7 percent is listed as miscellaneous agricultural products.[3] Therefore, one can conclude that a few types of commodities and large tonnages give the agency Żegluga na Odrze an advantage, in comparison with other inland water shippers, in that it can apply a greater degree of mechanization to the movement, thus decreasing the total cost of transfer. Unfortunately, statistical data showing rates and comparative cost for providing the service of transportation is not available to substantiate this assumption. Nevertheless, the relative importance of each group of commodity in inland waterway carriers can be shown by ranking their shipments according to tonnages. Table 5.3, lists a group of fourteen commodities carried by the agency Żegluga na Odrze according to rank. This ranking of Żegluga na Odrze can be compared with other agencies such as Żegluga Bydogska and, as one can see, these two show no parallelism. In comparing the year 1966 with 1970, one can notice on the Oder the continually increasing concentration in fewer commodities by large tonnages.

These obvious differences, between the agencies navigating Polish inland waterways in the type of commodity moved, leads one to question whether there are regional variations and differences on a small scale in the tonnages and the type of commodity carried within the Oder system. Thus one should ask the question: Is the Oder River, including the Gliwice Canal, along its entire length a homogeneous way from the point of type of commodity moved and traffic density? One could only assume that the differences in the quantity and the type of commodity offered for shipment would stem from regional differences. As has been discussed before, the quantitative and qualitative demands are derived demands which are generated from the needs within the

3
Ibid.

TABLE 5.3.

RELATIVE IMPORTANCE OF SHIPMENTS BY INLAND
WATERWAY ACCORDING TO AGENCIES

Commodity	Żegluga na Odrze Rank	Żegluga Bydgoska Rank	Rank on All of Poland's Inland Waterways
Bituminous Coal	1	-	2
Sand and Gravel	2	1	1
Ores	4	-	3
Fertilizer	3	6	5
Stone	6	7	4
Wood and Wood Products	10	10	6
Grain	5	5	7
Other Commodity	11	3	9
Cement	12	8	13
Lignite and Coke	9	-	12
Metals and Metal Products	7	9	10
Misc. Agricultural Products	8	2	8
Misc. Chemicals	13	4	11
Petroleum	14	-	14

Source: From the records of Główny Urząd Statystyczny, (Warsaw: 1971).

hinterland that the particular mode is serving.
Therefore, if significant variations and differences
exist within the hinterland that the particular mode
is serving, then the quantitative and qualitative
demand for movement would greatly differ from region
to region.

Type of Intraregional and Interregional Movement
Within the domestic inland water freight shipments,
one can distinguish two methods of moving a commodity
from the point of origin to the point of destination:

  1) Exclusively by inland waterways
  2) In combination barge-to-rail shipments
      a) with one transfer between modes
      b) with two transfers between modes.

134

Most of the tonnage carried by the state agency
Żegluga na Odrze is of the barge-to-rail combination
type. Actually, very little tonnage in Poland moves
exclusively from the point of origin to the final
destination by inland waterways. Surprisingly,
barge-to-truck shipments virtually do not exist on
the Oder. This perhaps stems from the lack of complementarity in the type of commodity moved in Poland
by the barge industry and the trucking industry.

The combination barge-to-rail shipments on the
Oder, measured in ton-kilometers, make up 82.0 percent
of the total commodity moved.[4] The national average
measured in ton-kilometers, for combination type of
movement, is 70.2 percent.[5] Looking at the actual
tonnages moved, one obtains a slightly different
picture. The actual tons of commodity moved by the
agency Żegluga na Odrze in combination barge-to-rail
shipments, constitutes only 64.9 percent of its
total tonnage.[6]

The differences in the measurement between ton-
kilometers and tonnages suggest that relatively few
types of high value commodities are shipped over long
distances. In both cases the Oder leads the nation
in combination barge-to-rail type of movement in this
region within the total transportation system.
Furthermore, the variations in the percentages of the
combination type of movement from one inland water
agency to another is also indicative of the type and
value of the commodity that is mostly carried by that
particular agency. The higher value commodity is more
transferable than low value commodity. Thus the

---

[4]
Ibid., Table 8, p. 5.

[5]
Ibid.

[6]
Ibid.

agency whose total make-up tonnage is of relatively low value per weight will exhibit a significantly smaller percentage of combination-type movement.

To exemplify this point, one can demonstrate that the agency Żegluga Bydgoska, whose 48.4 percent share of total tonnage in 1970 was composed of sand and gravel, combination barge-to-rail type of movement was only 38.5 percent of the total, measured in terms of ton-kilometers.[7] The same low percentage of combination-type movement in relation to total tonnages is also true in the case of the agency operating on the lower and middle Vistula, Żegluga Warszawska.

The combination-type shipments which are so prevalent on the Oder are primarily of that particular category representing one transfer between modes. Domestic shipments with two transfers between modes are considered most costly, requiring a greater output of capital and labor and, in recent years, statistics indicate that they are being phased out from the scene of interregional movement. A typical example of combination barge-to-rail shipment with two transfers is the movement of coking coal from the mines at Wałbrzych and coke from the processing plants to the steel plants in Upper Silesia. The coal from the mines is shipped by railroad to the port of Wrocław where it is loaded on barges to be moved up the river to the port of Gliwice. At this point, coking coal is unloaded from the barges to rail hoppers for shipment to its final place of destination. Reduction in shipments with two transfers between modes in recent years is reflected in the relative importance of some commodities in the make-up of total shipments. For example on the Oder in the past several years the share of bituminous and coking coal in relationship to the total tonnage moved decreased from 60 percent in 1960 to 51 percent in 1970. In spite of this decrease coal still occupies

[7]
Ibid.

first place, as one can see from Table 5.2. in the previous section, indicating the relative importance of various commodities in interregional movement on the Oder.

The only available statistical data on the intraregional movement of commodities via the Oder River, within the study area, is presented in Table 5.4. A close examination of the table reveals that intraregional movement by water carriers within the Oder hinterland to the total inland water movement was relatively high both in 1965 and 1967, 39.9 and 48 percent, respectively. In 1970, the intraregional traffic had significantly decreased to 43.1 percent of the total movement. If one examines Table 5.4. in conjunction with Figures 5.1. and 5.2., it can be seen that in the case of the individual województwo Szczecin, in addition to being the major receiver of goods from the other regions, 88.8 percent of the port of Szczecin's total consignment in 1970 was destined for shipment within the województwo itself. Surprisingly, the only other województwa which show any intraregional movement are Opole and Wrocław. The share of intraregional shipment to the total consignment in 1970 for Wrocław and Opole was 59.5 and 4.2 percent, respectively.

Looking at the interregional movement of a commodity via the Oder River, it can be seen that there is a marked increase from 1965 to 1970. The major shipper was województwo Katowice, whose entire inland shipments in 1970 were consigned for shipment outside of the boundaries of its respective region. The next closest regions with a large percentage of commodities shipped outside of the regions were województwo Opole and Wrocław.

The major receivers of commodities via inland waterways from other regions in 1970 were województwa Szczecin and Katowice and the city of Wrocław. By comparing Figures 5.1. and 5.2. it can be seen that województwo Katowice is both the major shipper of commodity outside of its own region and the major receiver from other regions.

If one looks at the last column of Table 5.4., which shows the balance between export and import for

TABLE 5.4.

INTRAREGIONAL AND INTERREGIONAL MOVEMENT OF COMMODITY
ON THE ODER FOR SELECTED YEARS (IN TONS)

Region	Year	Consigned			Received			Balance Export of Import
		Total	For Shipment Within Region	For Shipment Outside Region	Total	Shipment From Within Region	Shipment From Outside Region	
City of Wrocław	1965	266,185	25,850	240,335	209,129	25,850	183,279	57,056
	1967	157,895	10,901	146,994	543,620	10,901	532,719	-385,725
	1968	581,297	408,334	172,963	555,552	408,334	142,218	25,745
	1970	754,649	464,477	293,172	723,376	464,477	258,899	34,273
Katowice	1965	276,480	---	276,480	380,295	---	380,295	-103,815
	1967	551,068	---	551,068	467,201	---	467,201	83,867
	1968	621,188	---	621,188	571,455	---	571,455	49,733
	1970	984,390	---	984,390	563,313	---	563,313	421,077
Opole	1965	650,127	85,314	564,813	262,902	85,314	177,588	387,225
	1967	642,523	12,510	630,013	210,579	12,510	198,069	431,944
	1968	656,742	45,192	611,556	263,013	45,192	217,821	393,735
	1970	409,633	17,356	392,277	186,811	17,356	169,455	222,822
Szczecin	1965	623,506	620,447	3,059	1,271,096	620,447	650,649	-647,590
	1967	715,452	664,958	50,494	1,526,952	664,958	861,994	-811,500
	1968	868,808	790,536	78,272	1,479,969	790,536	689,443	-611,161
	1970	1,072,761	953,564	119,197	1,580,945	953,564	627,381	-508,184
Wrocław	1965	14,800	---	14,800	31,073	---	31,073	-16,273
	1967	415,049	8,865	406,184	54,849	8,865	45,984	360,200
	1968	33,267	---	33,267	44,793	---	44,793	-11,526
	1970	25,022	---	25,022	10,562	---	10,562	14,460
Zielona Góra	1965	4,421	---	4,421	16,596	---	16,596	-12,148
	1967	28,194	---	28,194	13,959	---	13,959	14,235
	1968	18,708	---	18,708	9,682	---	9,682	9,026
	1970	76,331	---	76,331	1,142	---	1,142	75,189

Source: Years 1965, 1967, and 1968 from Główny Urząd Statystyczny, Statystyka Żeglugi Śródlądowej (Warsaw: 1969), Table 19, p. 27; Year 1970 from the Office Zjednoczenie Żeglugi, Wrocław, July, 1971.

138

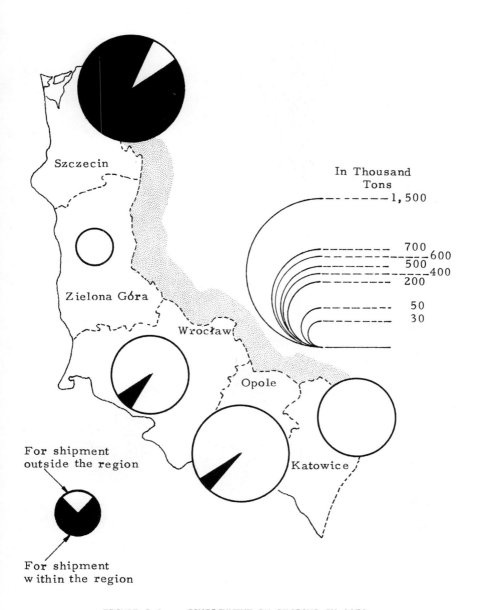

Szczecin

Zielona Góra

Wrocław

Opole

Katowice

In Thousand
Tons
1,500

700
600
500
400
200
50
30

For shipment
outside the region

For shipment
within the region

FIGURE 5.1.:   CONSIGNMENT BY REGIONS IN 1970

Source: Based on data in Table 5.4.

139

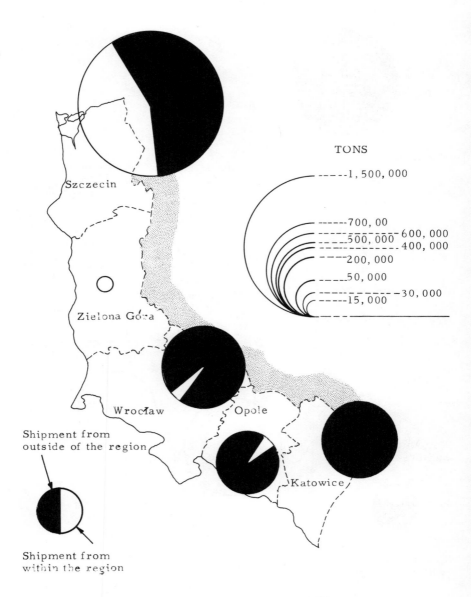

TONS

----1,500,000

-----700,00
------500,000-----600,000
-------------400,000
---200,000
---50,000
-----------30,000
---15,000

Szczecin

Zielona Góra

Wrocław   Opole

Shipment from
outside of the region

Katowice

Shipment from
within the region

FIGURE 5.2.:   SHIPMENT RECEIVED BY REGIONS IN 1970

Source: Based on data in Table 5.4.

140

individual regions, it can be seen that in 1970 the województwo of Katowice showed an excess of 421,077 tons of export over import, followed by Opole with 222,822 tons. In the same period, on the negative side where imports exceed exports, województwo Szczecin leads with 508,184 tons. Table 5.5. summarizes the relative importance of the województwo in interregional trade.

If one looks at the shipments by type of commodity by the agency Żegluga na Odrze one can see a great deal of difference between intraregional and interregional movement. In the three regions, Szczecin, Wrocław, and Opole, which are the only ones that show intraregional movement by inland waterways in Figure 5.3., the major commodity in 1970 was sand and gravel. This overwhelming importance of sand and gravel in intraregional movement by barges can be demonstrated by citing that in 1970, 92.3 percent of a total 1,435,397 tons, classified strictly as internal movement within each region, was sand and gravel.

The analysis of the table, which shows both intraregional and interregional movement by type of commodity, reveals that sand and gravel occupied a dominant but slightly different position in each region. It ranges from 100 percent of the total intraregional movement, as in the case of województwo Wrocław, to 85.3 and 82.1 percent in województwa Opole and Szczecin, respectively. The remaining barge tonnages of internal movement within the region is primarily wood and grain. The województwo of Szczecin is the only region within the study area that shows at least some degree of diversity in the type of commodity moved by barges within the region. This can be illustrated by indicating that in 1970, excluding wood and wood products and grain which were 6.6 percent and 3.5 percent, respectively, of the total intraregional barge tonnage, the remaining ten commodities within the list command less than 2.5 percent of the total.

The interregional movement of commodity by Żegluga na Odrze is more diversified than that of the intraregional. In the movement between regions, in addition to having greater diversity in the greater

141

TABLE 5.5.

RELATIVE IMPORTANCE OF REGIONS IN INTERREGIONAL TRADE
FOR 1965-1968-1970 (IN PERCENT OF TOTAL)

Region	1965		1968		1970	
	Export	Import	Export	Import	Export	Import
Total for the 6 regions (in 1,000 tons)	1,104	1,439	1,535	1,675	1,890	1,631
City of Wrocław	21.8	12.7	11.2	8.4	15.0	15.8
Katowice	25.0	26.4	40.4	34.0	52.0	34.5
Opole	51.2	12.3	39.8	7.0	20.7	10.3
Szczecin	0.3	45.2	5.0	41.1	6.2	38.4
Wrocław	1.3	2.2	2.1	2.6	1.3	0.6
Zielona Góra	0.4	1.2	1.2	0.5	4.0	0.4
	100.0%	100.0%	100.0%	100.0%	100.0%	100.0%

Source: Based on data in Table 5.4.

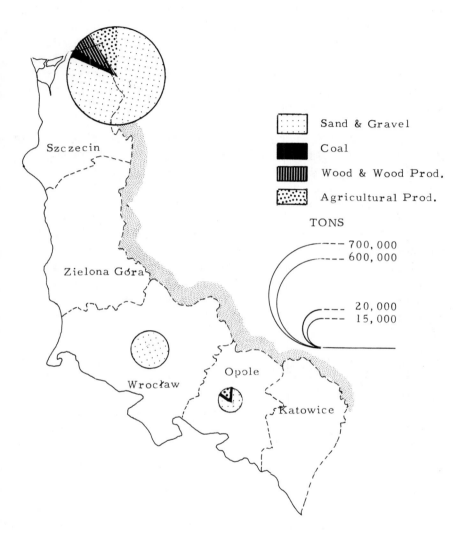

Szczecin

Zielona Góra

Wrocław

Opole

Katowice

Sand & Gravel

Coal

Wood & Wood Prod.

Agricultural Prod.

TONS

700,000
600,000

20,000
15,000

FIGURE 5.3.:   INTRAREGIONAL MOVEMENT BY TYPE OF COMMODITY IN 1970

Source: Based on statistics in Tables 1,2,3,4, and 5 in the Appendix

143

number of commodities shipped to total movement, one can also notice pronounced differences between the exports and imports of the individual regions. As one can see in Figure 5.4., the major share of exports of the southern województwa, Katowice, Opole, and Wrocław consists of coal, 95.8 percent, 70.6 percent, and 80.8 percent, respectively. The northern regions, Zielona Góra and Szczecin, are relatively small exporters of goods via inland waterways, however, they show a greater diversity in the type of commodity moved.

The largest single importer among the five regions is województwo Szczecin, coal occupying 71.5 percent of the total goods received. It is not suprising to find that natural resources such as various ores and sand and gravel occupy a high percent of the imports of województwa Opole and Katowice. In recent years, one can notice a sizable decline of sand and gravel in the make-up of interregional movement and the simultaneous rise in the importance of coal. This shift is a result of the technological improvements on the Oder and the search for an alternate link between Upper Silesia and the port of Szczecin in order to alleviate the heavy strain on the railroad.

International Movement

In the geographic and political systems of Central Europe in the Post-World War II period, the Oder waterway occupies an entirely different position from that of the Pre-1939 period. This river is thought of by the enthusiasts of inland water navigation within the Polish government and the neighboring riparian states, East Germany and Czechoslovakia, as a vital link of communication between socialist states and an essential implement in the building of socialism. Irrespective of whether one sees the river in the light of dialectic materialism, it would be interesting to analyze the function and relative importance of the Oder waterway in the international movement of commodity. The primary questions to be asked here are: What characterizes the movements of commodities to and from foreign countries? What is the quantitative and qualitative demand for this type

144

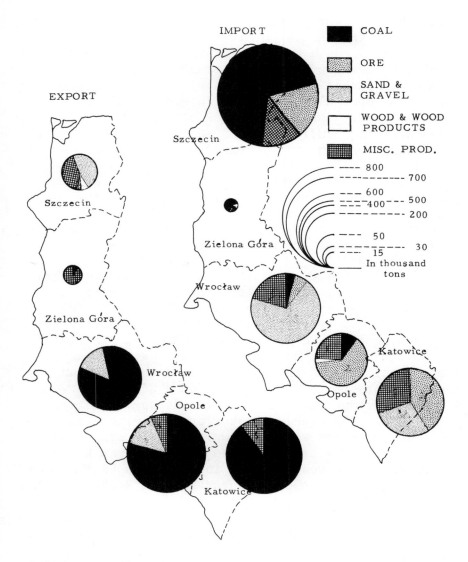

FIGURE 5.4.:   REGIONAL EXPORT - IMPORT BY TYPE OF COMMODITY IN 1970

Source: Based on statistics in Tables 1,2,3,4, and 5 in the Appendix

145

of movement? and: How does the international traffic differ from the domestic? It is quite possible, as in many other instances in socialist countries, that the rhetoric and optimism does not necessarily coincide with the hard economic reality.

Poland, as a country taking part in international trade by means of inland waterways, entered the European market relatively late,[8] in spite of the fact that the Oder River had been internationalized since World War I. The Soviet block countries prior to the death of Stalin in 1953, in conjunction with Moscow's foreign policy, practiced political and economic isolation from the rest of the world. The Oder River basin, approximately 90 percent of it being within the territory of Poland, gave the Polish authorities absolute control over navigation. This policy of selective isolationism, however, drastically changed with the new winds of the "thaw" which blew from the east.

In 1954, the first shipments destined for the Western European markets via the Oder waterway were recorded. Goods dispatched during the years 1954 and 1955 were confined exclusively to commodity exchange, between Poland and West Germany. In the case of Socialist countries, on the basis of an agreement between the Polish and Czechoslovakian governments in 1948, the Oder for a period of several years became a transit waterway for Czechoslovakia. The agency, Ceskoslovenska Plavba Labsko-Oderska with its main headquarters in Prague, and its own river fleet navigated the Oder from Koźle to Sczcecin. Two years later, in 1950, the East German state agency, Deutsche Binnenschiffart Reederei, also began navigation on the Oder.

Further expansion of the international traffic on the Oder and Central European inland waterways was introduced in 1960. In the spirit of peaceful coexistence with the West and the realization of the

---

8
The Oder River had been internationalized by the Versailles Treaty of 1918.

profitability of trade between east and west, several commercial agreements between Poland, West Berlin and Holland were concluded. Two years later, in 1962, Belgium entered on the scene, becoming an important consumer of Polish agricultural products and semi-finished manufactured goods. It is interesting to note, however, that since 1962 the number of countries taking part in the exchange of commodities with Poland via the Oder waterway and the connected systems of inland waterways has not drastically changed to the present day.

The Oder River, as shown in Figure 5.5., is tied by an intricate and well-developed system of canals with the major rivers of Europe such as the Elbe, Weser, and Rhine. Due to the fact that the Oder is the eastern extremity of the great European inland waterway system, Poland is capable of exchanging commodity with most of the industrialized countries of Europe. The navigable rivers of Western Europe have been in the past and persist to be more influential as locational magnets in attracting heavy industry to their shores than has been true in the case of Poland. Consequently, the industrial might of Western Europe is quite accessible by the European inland water system and their carriers have always played an important role in moving commodities, both on the concentration and the dispersal sides. Only recently, in the wake of renewed interest in Poland's inland waterways and the subsequent rejuvenation of the barge industry as a mode of transportation, are inland waterways beginning to play a role in locational decisions of that country.

Unfortunately, at the present time, the inland water connections between the Oder River and the rest of the European inland waterway system are less than satisfactory. The initial objective and energy should be directed to the improvement of the east-west connections between northerly flowing rivers which are the primary directional demand for movement within this region. For the Oder to play a significant role in international movement of commodity, it must be fully integrated into the rest of the European inland water system. Prior to the intervention by

147

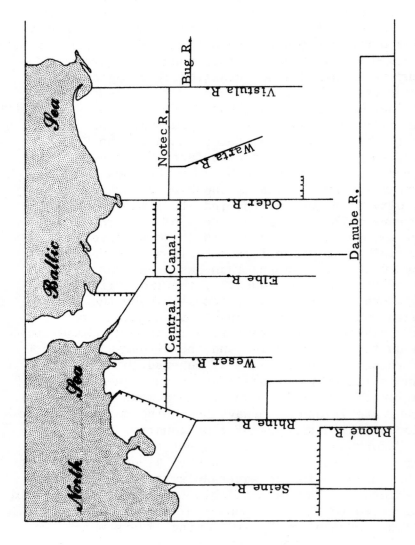

FIGURE 5.5.: SCHEMATIC CHART OF THE NAVIGABLE RIVERS AND CANALS OF EUROPE

the Warsaw Pact countries in Czechoslovakia, there
had been expressed interest by Polish and Czechoslovakian planners in linking the Oder with the Elbe and
Danube Rivers which, in turn, would provide an inland
connection between the Baltic and Black Seas.[9]

Looking at the Oder River as an artery of transportation beyond the confines of the national framework of Polish economy, it can be said that it has
the potential and the possibility of becoming an
international inland waterway of some consequence.
The Oder River, due to its excellent geographic location, aligned along a north-south axis, constitutes
the shortest and simplest water connection between
the Baltic, through the Elbe and Danube Rivers, with
the Black Sea. In addition, by linking the West
European inland water system with that of the Soviet
Union, the Oder's present peripheral position would
change to that of a central one. Thus the Oder River,
in spite of its adverse physical peculiarities but
with major technical improvements, could become the
keystone in the whole European inland waterway
system, serving in this function not only the countries
of COMECON but Western Europe as well.

At the conference held in Koźle in July, 1968, by
parties interested in expanding navigation on the
Oder, mainly Poland and Czechoslovakia, ambitious
plans were drawn to begin construction of the Oder-
Danube Canal and to fully modernize the Oder. It
was hoped that this river could truly become an
international artery of transportation. However,
the tragic events in Czechoslovakia, which shortly
followed after the conclusion of the conference, dis-
rupted any further talks and cooperation regarding
the Oder River.

At the present, international freight traffic
on the Oder River consists of three distinctive types
of movement which are: imports to Poland, exports
from Poland, and transit through Polish territory to

---

[9]
 Kazimierz Puczynski, "Kanal Odra-Dunaj," Gospodarka Wodna, Nr. 6 (June,
1968), p. 216.

and from neighboring countries. In aggregate these three types of movements, which are distinctively classified as international traffic, are relatively small in comparison to the total tonnage on the Oder, however, with each successive year the international traffic assumes greater importance. At the beginning of Poland's participation in 1954, in international trade via inland waterways, international traffic on the Oder, measured in actual tons carried, was less than 10 percent of the total tonnage.[10] After eleven years, by 1965, it rose to 18.3 percent of the total tonnage and in 1970 it rose to a new high of 31.1 percent.[11]

If one compares the annual rise of international inland water traffic to the rise of total Polish inland water traffic, it can be seen that there is a great deal of parallelism. The international freight traffic rose on the average approximately 8 percent from 1954 to 1970, while total domestic traffic on the Oder rose 7.1 percent for the same period. Looking at the individual components of the international traffic, it can be seen from Table 5.6. that exports from Poland in two periods, 1965 and 1968, exceeded imports by approximately 50 percent. In 1970 exports comprised 30.1 percent of the total international freight tonnages, whereas imports commanded 27.8 percent, thus one can see a greater degree of balance between imports and exports in the latter year.

The largest and most important component of international freight traffic on the Oder is the transit movement. In 1965 it consisted of 53.6 percent of the total foreign tonnage. It is interesting to note that in 1970 international traffic rose sharply from the previous two year period by 39.7 percent. However, in relative terms to the total foreign traffic, the transit traffic in 1970 declined in comparison with 1968 traffic by 1.4 percent. In

[10]
Główny Urząd Statystyczny, Rocznik Statystyczny Transportu 1945-1966 (Warsaw: 1967), p. 499.

[11]
Percentages calculated from the data in Table 5.6.

TABLE 5.6.

INTERNATIONAL FREIGHT MOVEMENT ON THE ODER
FOR SELECTED YEARS (IN TONS)

Type of Movement	1965	1968	1970
Total Freight Movement on the Oder	2,052,390	2,795,041	3,133,027
Total International Freight Movement	375,996	570,057	975,812
Imports (to Poland)	50,063	92,795	272,031
Exports (from Poland)	107,252	186,868	293,904
Transit	201,644	247,353	409,841

Sources: Years 1965 and 1968 from Główny Urząd Statystyczny, Statystyka Żeglugi
Śródlądowej i Dróg Wodnych Śródlądowych 1968, Nr. 48 (Warsaw: 1969), Tables 10
and 11, pp. 7-8; Year 1970 from the records of Żegluga na Odrze, Wrocław, July,
1971.

1970 transit traffic constituted only 41.9 percent of
the total international traffic. The explanation for
this continuous decline of transit traffic on the
Oder is that Czechoslovakia in recent years has ceased
navigation altogether on the Oder while securing more
accessible and, thus, more economical routes for her
exports via West European ports. For example, in
1970 the port of Hamburg was receiving four times as
much Czechoslovakian transit as the port of Szczecin.
Here is a prime example where economic considerations,
price incentives, and self-interest of the nation
state, even in this Socialist system, prevails over
the ideological commitments.

The river port at Koźle, in some degree continues
to be an important transshipment port for the remaining Czechoslovakian transit. Freight in transit
to and from Czechoslovakia is carried by the boats
of the agency Żegluga na Odrze. The Czechoslovakian
transit carried by Polish barges is predominantly

raw materials, such as iron ore, phosphite, and periodotite. These raw materials are loaded directly into barges from ocean bottoms in the maritime port of Szczecin and the barges then proceed up river to Koźle where trans-loading into railroad cars takes place for the remaining journey to the point of destination. This procedure is reversed for some Czechoslovakian export which is predominantly manufactured and semi-finished goods. In spite of the gradually declining Czechoslovakian transit carried by Żegluga na Odrze, Polish planners are quite optimistic in thinking that with the modernization of the Oder waterway and the constantly rising demands in Czechoslovakia for raw materials, especially in the Ostrava-Karvina manufacturing district, the transit movement on the Oder will have no other choice but to increase.[12] Thus with the modernization of the Oder River to comparable standards of other European navigable rivers and, particularly with the extension of the navigable channel to the city of Ostrava, great possibilities can be seen for Czechoslovakian transit. One would hope that not only freight traffic can be redirected to take the most direct route between this industrial complex and the maritime port but, also, differential rates between railroads and inland water carriers for bulk commodity will be a proper cost incentive leading to the greater utilization of the latter.

In many instances the reluctance on the part of the shippers to use the services of the water carriers is directly related to the physical and technological conditions of the inland waterways which affects the level of service. Therefore, if these structural obstacles in the routeway can be eliminated by technological improvements then, at least, this mode of transportation, where ever it is accessible, can become more competitive, if not exclusively exercising an absolute advantage in the movement of bulk commodity.

[12]
Based on the author's interview with the officials of Żegluga na Odrze, Wrocław, July, 1971.

In the case of Poland's imports and exports, it is interesting to note in Table 5.7. that imports from West Germany via inland waterways rose considerably from 21.5 percent of the total Polish imports in 1965, to 48.5 and 50.2 percent in 1968 and 1970, respectively. At the same time, one can see that Holland and West Germany are the major receivers of Polish goods exported via inland waterways. Here one can suggest some degree of complementarity between these respective countries which always preempts the conditions for trade.

Examination of the qualitative demands show that, as in the case of domestic traffic, in international movements the Oder River is a carrier of bulk commodities and the range of goods approximates that of the domestic movement. In this respect there is a great deal of parallelism between domestic and international movement. As one can see in Table 5.8., earlier there was a complete lack of a concentration of large tonnages in a few commodities in both periods, 1965 and 1968. Instead, one sees a more or less even distribution of total tonnage among the twelve commodities listed. In comparing the year 1965 with that of 1968, it can be seen that in 1965 coal was the primary commodity carried by the inland waterways, 37.1 percent of the total international tonnage. In 1968, however, shipments were more diversified and the share that coal occupied in the international movement dropped significantly to 16.2 percent of the total tonnage. In domestic traffic, as has been noted, sand and gravel held second position in tonnages carried on the Oder River, however, in the international movement the table below shows that sand and gravel constituted only 2.0 percent of the total tonnage in 1968. If one compares the year 1968 with that of 1970, one notices the re-emergence of concentration in three basic commodities, such as coal, fertilizer, and ores. In 1970 coal, once again, became the primary commodity in the international movement with 43.5 percent of the total foreign traffic, to be followed by fertilizer and ores, 22.3 and 17.6 percent respectively. A low value commodity sand reached a new ebb, 1.1 percent of the total tonnage.

153

TABLE 5.7.

RELATIVE IMPORTANCE OF NATIONS PARTICIPATING IN
FOREIGN TRADE WITH POLAND VIA INLAND WATERWAYS

Country	Import To Poland						Export From Poland					
	1965	%	1968	%	1970	%	1965	%	1968	%	1970	%
Total Tons	50,063 = 100.0		92,795 = 100.0		272,031 = 100.0		107,252 = 100.0		186,868 = 100.0		293,904 = 100.0	
Belgium		8.0		3.0		3.5		7.2		11.4		13.1
France		---		13.0		12.9		---		0.9		2.1
Holland		28.3		12.7		15.3		20.0		22.5		24.9
East Germany		42.2		22.8		18.1		20.5		12.9		14.7
West Germany		21.5		48.5		50.2		22.7		23.5		20.5

Sources: Years 1965 and 1968 from Główny Urząd Statystyczny, Statystyka Żeglugi Śródlądowej (Warsaw: 1969), Table 11, p. 8; Year 1970 from the records of Żegluga na Odrze, Wrocław, June, 1971.

154

TABLE 5.8.

INTERNATIONAL MOVEMENT BY TYPE OF COMMODITY
FOR SELECTED YEARS (EXPORT-IMPORT)

Commodity	In Tons		
	1965	1968	1970
Total	157,315	279,663	565,935
Coal	58,450	45,312	243,352
Ores	---	16,163	101,868
Stone	20,662	45,282	20,939
Sand and Gravel	11,563	5,852	6,225
Metals and Metal Products	7,838	40,350	23,224
Cement	1,197	17,521	2,829
Fertilizer	22,500	37,922	126,203
Miscellaneous Chemicals	1,474	3,645	6,227
Grain	15,471	9,844	15,846
Misc. Agricultural Products	7,947	31,410	17,544
Wood and Wood Products	5,334	16,958	1,698
Other Commodities	4,879	9,404	6,791

Sources: Years 1965 and 1968 from Główny Urząd Statystyczny, Statystyka Żeglugi Śródlądowej i Dróg Wodnych Śródlądowych 1968, Nr. 48 (Warsaw: 1969), Table 12, p. 8,;
Year 1970 from the records of Żegluga na Odrze, Wrocław, July, 1971.

As a result of the economic reforms in the 1960's, the greater emphasis on cost accounting and the encouraged competition between carriers in Poland makes long hauls, of a commodity whose value per weight is relatively low, economically prohibitive. Therefore, it is not surprising to find that, as in the case of domestic movement, the international movement of sand and gravel over a long distance does not take place. One obvious distinction between domestic and international movement via inland waterways is that the international movement is marked by much longer hauls for the individual type of commodity.

Functional Analysis of Movement

The analysis of intraregional and interregional freight movement on the Oder River reveals that goods will move through the inland water network from the points of origin to the points of destination by a somewhat specified distance and predictable direction. This suggests, perhaps, that the Oder waterway can be divided, based on direction and distance of movement, into easily identifiable major functional sectors. As a result of the fundamental differences between domestic and international freight traffic, in the points of origin and destination and subsequent differences in the direction, distance, and the pattern of movement, the network through which the commodities move must also be different.

In other words, these two networks could not possibly be identical, as each one has its distinctive focal points which are connected into a circulatory system by different sizes and types of links, thus creating its own distinctive network pattern. This does not negate the fact, however, that one can find and expect to find a certain degree of similarity and overlap through common points within these two networks. Therefore, the functional sectors within the network which can be identified and delimited for domestic traffic could have a certain degree of similarity, but will not necessarily coincide with those of the international sectors.

First, the domestic freight traffic is examined from points of origin to the points of destination to

156

determine whether some form of a functional division of the Oder inland waterway exists. Based on this examination, one can recognize two major distinctive sectors. The first sector is Gliwice to Wrocław and the second one is Wrocław to Szczecin. In addition, the first sector can be further subdivided into functional subsectors. Consequently, one can obtain the following functional division of the Oder waterway which is illustrated in Figure 5.6.

Sector I Gliwice-Wrocław
    a) Gliwice-Koźle
    b) Koźle-Wrocław
Sector II Wrocław-Szczecin

It is not surprising that these individual sectors, with their subsectors, converge on and at the same time are separated from each other by major river ports. In this case, the river ports not only serve as a nodal point where modes of transportation come together but also as separators of various movements.

The few available figures on intercity movement of commodity by the agency Żegluga na Odrze emphasize the importance of the great river ports such as Gliwice, Wrocław, and Szczecin. Each one of these major ports are the beginning and/or end of a functional line of the Oder's inland water system. Each one of these sectors of the Oder's waterway system, identified above, has its own distinctive characteristics and idiosyncrasies relating to volume of traffic, diversity in commodity, and direction of movement.

The first sector, Gliwice-Wrocław, has high densities as its regions, województwa Katowice, Opole, and Wrocław, generate large volumes of traffic. Large volumes but a small number of commodities, such as raw materials and finished manufactured goods, are moved between the end terminals of this sector. This sector is further divided by the port of Koźle, whose primary function is a point of transshipment from barge to railroad and vice versa, into two subsectors each with its own distinctive characteristics. The smaller ports within the Gliwice-Wrocław sector such as Opole and Oława play only secondary roles.

157

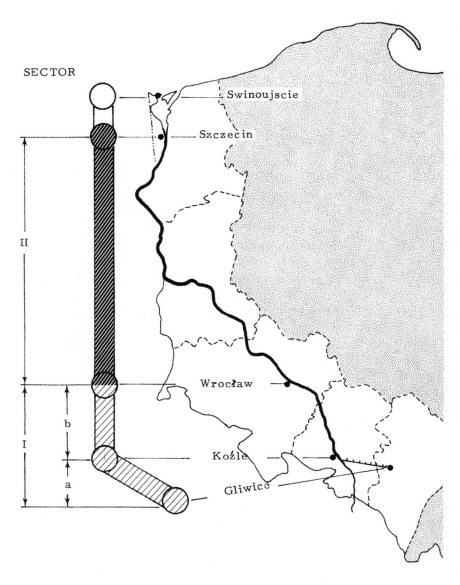

FIGURE 5.6.: FUNCTIONAL DIVISION OF THE ODER WATERWAY BASED ON
              DOMESTIC TRAFFIC MOVEMENT

The second sector, Wrocław-Szczecin, is significantly longer and more diversified. It performs an explicitly throughway function. Along the way, from Wrocław to Szczecin, there are no major ports of transshipment. From the point of strictly national traffic, this sector actually ends at the port of Szczecin. To Swinoujscie, 60 kilometers north of Szczecin on the island of Uznam, the only movement consists of that portion of coal which is consigned for export to Sweden. There it is transloaded into deep draft bottoms for the further journey via the Baltic Sea. Therefore, the segment, Szczecin to Swinoujscie, cannot be included within the domestic transportation system. The województwo Szczecin receives large volumes of commodities from Upper and Lower Silesia, not only for eventual export to foreign markets, but also for consumption and processing of raw materials in the local iron and steel, chemical, and energy generating industries which cluster around the city of Szczecin.

In analyzing the directional movement of international shipments, the division of the Oder waterway into functional segments appears to be entirely different from that of domestic traffic. As is shown in Figure 5.7., one may distinguish five sectors:

Sector   I   Gliwice-Wrocław
                a) Gliwice-Koźle
                b) Koźle-Wrocław
Sector   II   Wrocław-Przybrzeg
Sector III   Przybrzeg-Cedynia
Sector   IV   Cedynia-Szczecin
Sector   V   Szczecin-Swinoujscie.

This diverse division of the Oder waterway is a result of differences in the characteristics of foreign commodities flow. The important fact, in this functional division of the Oder waterway, is the directional flow of goods between the points of origin and the destinations. It should be pointed out that the movement of goods on the Oder itself, in the case of international traffic, measured in time or actual kilometers in relation to the total journey, is relatively small. For example, on the journey from

159

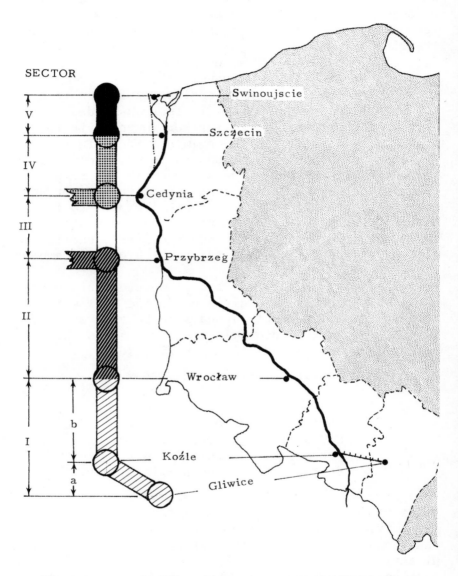

FIGURE 5.7.: FUNCTIONAL DIVISION OF THE ODER WATERWAY BASED ON INTERNATIONAL TRAFFIC MOVEMENT

160

Wrocław to Amsterdam by inland waterways less than 3 percent of the total travel time is spent on the Oder.[13] Thus the Oder in this movement becomes a relatively small segment within the larger network.

The importance of the direction of commodity flow, as a factor in the functional division of the Oder waterway, can be exemplified by citing two typical movements. For example, barges destined for West Berlin, Magdeburg, and the southern portion of West Germany will move by the Oder to Przybrzeg where they will enter the Oder-Spree Canal and proceed to their final destination through the inland waterway network of East and West Germany. Meanwhile, barges consigned for Hamburg, Holland, and Belgium, will move by the Oder to Cedynia where they will enter the Oder-Havel Canal. Thus, as a result of these two distinctive directional movements in international trade, one can identify two functional segments in the middle Oder, Wrocław-Przybrzeg and Przybrzeg-Cedynia.

Because Wrocław and Gliwice are the most important transshipment ports for both domestic and international traffic in the Oder network, the portion of the waterway which connects these two ports must be considered, in both cases, as a functional sector. These ports are either points of origin of commodities destined for export, such as coal from Upper Silesia loaded at Gliwice, or points of destination for imports from Western Europe. The ports of Gliwice and Wrocław are the focal points for both domestic and foreign traffic. Here the two systems come together and overlap on common points. So far the three functional segments on the Oder were obtained as a result of the peculiarities of the outward movement of Poland's exports.

The fourth segment, Cedynia-Szczecin, is a result of the return flow of a single commodity, Hardwood imported from Holland moves through a network of mid-western canals and enters the Oder River at

---

[13]
Lucjan Hofman, Ekonomica Branżowa Jako Nauka (Sopot: Wyższa Szkoła Ekonomiczna 1962), p. 124.

Cedynia and proceeds north to the woodworking plants at Szczecin. This segment, in comparison to the other three, has the least traffic density because, aside from hardwood, little or no other imports or exports are moved through this sector. The last segment, the smallest of all, Szczecin to Swinoujscie, as has already been discussed results from the movement of Silesian coal for export to Sweden.

The analysis of domestic and international traffic and their respective functional divisions into segments suggest that both divisions should be compared. The question asked here is: What are the similarities and differences between these two divisions? In the course of the examination of similarities and differences between national and international movements, particularly in view of the lack of statistical data which would permit a more quantitative analysis, one is forced to make only a few superficial generalizations. Whatever the shortcomings of these generalizations are, they should still shed some light on the idiosyncrasies of both types of movements.

In the sector Gliwice to Wrocław, a sector of high traffic densities, there is a great deal of similarity between domestic and international movement. As one can see, the sector Gliwice to Wrocław continues to be subdivided into two functional subsectors. Beyond this portion of the waterway, the similarities between national and international traffic cease to exist. The second major sector, Wrocław to Szczecin, which appears as a throughway segment in the inter-regional domestic movement of commodity, does not exist in the case of international movement. Instead, this portion of the waterway from Wrocław to Szczecin is divided into three equal sectors with their own characteristics and idiosyncrasies. The last sector of the Oder, Szczecin to Swinoujscie which continues to play only a secondary role in the international movement, does not appear at all in the domestic division.

In summary, one can say that as it appears from this functional analysis of both domestic and international movement, the Oder River is not a

162

transportation artery of uniform traffic densities and the intensity and direction of movement differs from the domestic to that of the international. In comparing the physical division of the Oder waterway with the functional, it can be said that there is surprisingly some degree of similarity. For example, the sector Gliwice to Koźle appears in both the physical and functional divisions. Moving further down the river we have the channelized sector of the Oder from Koźle to Brzeg Dolny, this sector is somewhat longer than the functional sector, extending beyond the city of Wrocław.

At the city of Wrocław, the similarities between the physical and functional divisions end. The segment of river from Brzeg-Dolny to Szczecin, the freely flowing Oder, has been described as the least suitable for the purpose of navigation, nevertheless, from the city of Wrocław one can distinguish three functional sectors in the network.

It is possible from the discussion of the above similarities and differences between the physical and functional division of the Oder River to deduct two conclusions. One may say, first, that the present movement of commodities on the Oder waterway are not determined largely, at least at this point, on the navigational conditions of the routeway. Secondly, the sectors which are better suited for navigation and the port facilities are not utilized to their optimum capacity in order to accentuate the physical differences in the Oder River network. Because tonnages on the Oder, at the present time, are relatively small, there are no significant differences in the intensity of traffic volume on the individual sectors. Thus one may accept both generalizations as valid. In the near future, with a rise in the volume of traffic, one can expect that the physical differences of the Oder waterway will be accentuated and intensity of movement will tend to reflect these physical limitations.

Chapter VI

The Oder River and Economic Development Within the Five Regions

The function of a transportation mode is to provide time and place utility. In technologically advanced societies, regardless of their political and economic systems, in order to utilize the economic resources to their greatest advantage in the production of goods and services, the basic question faced by transportation agencies is invariably: How much transportation service does each sector of the economy need? Thus it is not surprising to note that even in a planned socialist economy such as Poland, during a period of economic growth, the question of increments in the demand for and the supply of transportation services assumed critical importance. Therefore, the logical answer to the above-stated question in the planned economy may, just as in the free economy, have to be based on past, present and anticipated relationships between activity within the regions in each sector of the economy on the one hand, and transportation output measures on the other. Among the problems facing transportation geographers in Poland, some have particular significance since they are connected with the specific conditions of economic development.

In this chapter, first, an examination is made whether such relationships between the industrial sectors of the Polish economy in the study area and the volume of freight traffic on the river actually exists. For that reason, if one in evaluating various demands for transportation on the Oder would compare rates of growth in the value of production, within the five regions, with rates of growth in freight traffic on the river, the relationship between the two aggregates can be established.

164

The material to be set forth below, while it would be quite inadequate for a thorough analysis of detailed relationships, should nevertheless, reveal overall parallelism in growth trends for the two aggregates. If there are, as one would expect, stable relationships between the physical volume of freight traffic on the Oder, then it would be desirable to undertake a more detailed analysis. Secondly, the question is asked whether a transport-output correlative relationship exists for individual type commodities, such as coal, iron ore, fertilizers, and agricultural products. This analysis is undertaken because one may speculate that if one is able to establish the growth of the individual commodity and its demand for inland water transportation, then this would be a useful instrument in the planning and future development of the navigation on the Oder.

Method of Analysis

At first glance the growth of traffic on the Oder and industrial output in Poland shows a great deal of parallelism. If one assumes that the foremost objective of any statistical investigation, in geography or any other discipline, is to forecast one variable in terms of another, then it would be highly desirable to estimate a formal relationship between waterborne traffic on the Oder and the rate of industrialization.

First, for the purpose of this study, a simple regression analysis is used to determine the "best" fit for a given functional relationship. With the help of the method of least squares, the author will strive in this chapter to explain variation in the dependent variable, which is the freight traffic on the Oder, by variations in the independent variable, industrial output. Therefore, if the two variables, y (freight traffic on the Oder) and x (industrial output) are linearly related, the equation expressing this relationship will be of the following form:

$$y = B_0 + B_1 x.$$

165

B_1 is the parameter expressing the slope of the line and B_0 is the parameter which tells at what value the straight line cuts the axis of the y. The slope B_1 tells by how much y increases for an increase of unity of the value of x. Before one can employ the method of least squares, however, there are two assumptions that must be made. First, one must assume that the independent variable, industrial output, is measured without an error. Second, one must assume that for a given x (industrial output) there exists a normal and independent distribution of y (freight traffic on the Oder) values with mean,

$$B_0 + B_1 x = \mu \; y/x \text{ and variance } \sigma_E{}^2.$$

As we previously assumed, the demand for transportation is a derived demand which stems from geographically removed places of production and consumption. An additional factor is that the variances for each distribution associated with each x value must be assumed equal. The least square estimators of B_0 and B_1 are:

$$\hat{B}_0 = \overline{Y} - \overline{X}b$$

$$\hat{B}_1 = \frac{\sum\limits_{i=1}^{n}(Xi - \overline{X})(Yi - \overline{Y})}{\sum\limits_{i=1}^{n}(Xi - \overline{X})^2}$$

These estimators will give a fit leveling to a minimum unexplained variance. Success in fitting will be measured in terms of the coefficient of determination, r^2,

$$r^2 = \frac{\text{Explained Variance}}{\text{Total Variance}} \text{ x } 100 \text{ percent},$$

100 percent being a perfect fit and zero percent indicating that the fit of the regression line is so poor that the knowledge of x will in no way aid in the forecasting of y.

Secondly, a coefficient of linear multiple correlation is employed which can be expressed in the following formula:

$$r_{12.3} = \frac{r_{12} - r_{13}r_{23}}{\sqrt{(1 - r_{13}^2)(1 - r_{23}^2)}}$$

which measures the correlation between x_1 and y independently of x_2.

The subscripts refer to the three variables, x_1 (output), y (traffic), and x_2 (industrial index). This means that one can keep one variable constant, for example x_2 and find the coefficient of partial correlation between x_1 and y. This was introduced for the express purpose of differentiating between correlation of two variables as separate entities and two variables with an interdependence on the third variable which one chose to hold constant.

Relation Amoung Aggregates

In the following pages, an examination is made of the relationship between aggregate freight traffic on all Polish rivers, freight traffic on the Oder, and the total industrial output. The degree of parallelism in the trends of growth of the total freight traffic on the Oder and the total industrial output is brought out here through the use of a linear equation. As a measure of total industrial output, the author calculated the index of the Gross National Product which can be considered the only available indicator of the growth of Polish industrial output. The total ton-kilometers of freight traffic on all Polish rivers and freight traffic on the Oder and their total growth is shown in Table 6.1.

A regression analysis between these two aggregates, the index of industrial output and freight traffic on the Oder, was run on a 360 IBM computer and the results with their co-variations are very significant. As one can see in Figure 6.1. straight lines have been separately fitted and inserted on the chart for the two periods, 1946 to 1959 and 1960 to

TABLE 6.1.

INDEX OF GROSS NATIONAL PRODUCT AND GROWTH
OF INLAND WATER TRAFFIC IN POLAND AND THE ODER RIVER

Year	Rise of Poland's Gross National Product	Growth of Inland Waterway Traffic on all Polish Rivers in Million Ton-Km.	Growth of Traffic on the Oder in Thousand Ton-Km.
1946	100.0 Index	53.5	44,405
1947	133.3	69.7	59,245
1948	182.6	227.2	193,120
1949	222.3	334.4	284,240
1950	284.0	264.5	222,180
1951	346.7	340.6	286,104
1952	412.2	559.1	464,053
1953	484.2	597.1	793,910
1954	539.3	576.9	490,365
1955	600.9	775.0	643,250
1956	655.0	628.2	533,970
1957	719.9	708.1	601,885
1958	790.8	695.7	570,474
1959	863.5	639.4	530,702
1960	959.0	904.3	759,612
1961	1047.8	855.3	709,899
1962	1147.9	821.7	657,360
1963	1210.3	1025.8	841,156
1964	1323.4	1247.7	1,035,591
1965	1442.3	1409.3	1,121,187
1966	1562.6	1761.7	1,367,082
1967	1685.4	1881.4	1,432,535
1968	1786.5	2020.7	1,502,225
1969	1863.8	1621.6	958,815
1970	2070.5	2171.9	1,655,500

GROSS NATIONAL PRODUCT calculated as a sum of the following elements:
    a)   sale value of industrial goods and services
    b)   value of finished product, semi-finished, and unfinished production
        plus the value of means of production
    c)   value of consumed resources.

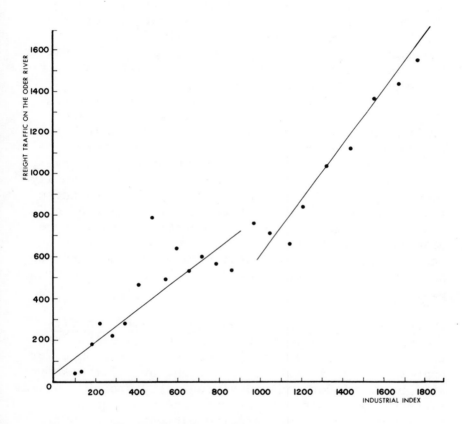

FIGURE 6.1.:   CORRELATIVE RELATIONSHIP BETWEEN FREIGHT TRAFFIC ON THE
ODER RIVER AND INDUSTRIAL OUTPUT

169

1970. It can be seen that not all observations lie
close to the two straight lines.

The least squares line fitted to observations
for 1946 to 1959 has the equation $Y = 66.66 + .87 X$
where x is industrial output and y is freight traffic.
The average absolute percentage deviation of actual
from predicted values over these fourteen years is
4.2 percent. The record for the later period, after
the reconstruction and the improvements in the physical facilities on the Oder is significantly better.
The equation $Y = 790.81 + 1.56 X$ fits the observations
from 1960 through 1970 with an average absolute percentage deviation of 2.3 percent.

The findings below indicate that the relationship between industrial production and aggregate
freight traffic on the Oder River, particularly in
the 1959 to 1970 period, is a close one indeed; the
value of r is .7728. It is not surprising, however,
that large economic aggregates are at least casually
connected through time and technology because these
massive composites are but two facets of a single
industrial process. Even if the success would have
been limited, the experiment above suggests that one
has here a useful instrument for projecting into the
near future, at least, observed relationships in the
past.

Correlative Relationships for Individual Commodity

The preceding examination of the aggregate freight
traffic and total industrial output gives ground for
hope that significant transport-output relationships
will be found for individual commodity groups. As raw
materials for these comparisons one needs annual output figures for representative elements in as many
commodity groups as possible with the freight traffic
records on the Oder. Table 6.2. presents annual data
for the years 1957 through 1970, covering the physical
output of coal, iron ore, fertilizer, and agricultural
products. Table 6.3. presents freight traffic records
on the Oder for these commodities. These four commodities were chosen because in total they represent 90
percent of all the traffic moved by the agency Żegluga
na Odrze. Examination of the correlative relationship

170

TABLE 6.2.

OUTPUT OF COAL, IRON ORE, FERTILIZER, AND
AGRICULTURAL PRODUCTS 1957-1970
(IN THOUSAND TONS)

Year	Coal	Iron Ore	Fertilizer	Agricultural Products
1957	94,096	1,785	2,081	44,582
1958	94,981	1,962	2,186	49,675
1959	99,106	2,014	2,285	54,347
1960	104,438	2,182	2,604	62,926
1961	106,606	2,386	2,888	72,763
1962	109,604	2,436	3,281	61,817
1963	113,150	2,609	3,402	70,589
1964	117,354	2,680	3,933	74,423
1965	118,831	2,861	4,329	71,917
1966	122,000	3,053	4,619	75,687
1967	124,000	3,077	5,209	80,600
1968	127,720	3,139	5,834	85,436
1969	130,400	3,168	6,395	90,216
1970	135,025	3,458	7,046	95,300

Sources: Główny Urząd Statystyczny, Rocznik Statystyczny Przemysłu 1945-1965 (Warsaw: 1967), Table 29, pp. 188-189; Główny Urząd Statystyczny, Rocznik Statystyczny Przemysłu 1967 (Warsaw, 1968), Table 29, pp. 201-202; Data for 1968, 1969, and 1970 from the office of Główny Urząd Statystyczny, Warsaw.

TABLE 6.3.

INLAND WATER FREIGHT TRAFFIC BY MAJOR COMMODITY
1957-1970
(IN THOUSAND OF METRIC TON-KILOMETERS)

Year	Coal	Iron Ore	Fertilizer	Agricultural Products
1957	351,580	146,250	76,515	59,235
1958	289,667	166,028	76,166	65,170
1959	241,212	130,734	62,176	62,450
1960	299,243	192,903	102,093	89,181
1961	256,033	189,596	76,461	92,234
1962	234,653	166,732	103,148	81,620
1963	343,932	225,737	127,208	80,227
1964	402,043	356,551	151,218	74,871
1965	454,370	376,170	176,336	129,356
1966	621,208	479,350	188,345	112,160
1967	727,272	475,528	176,318	82,872
1968	827,789	421,523	276,494	111,984
1969	643,822	259,563	223,673	94,625
1970	967,477	434,720	307,418	130,247

Sources: Główny Urząd Statystyczny, Rocznik Statystyczny Transportu 1945-1966 (Warsaw: 1967), Table 5, pp. 496-497; Data for 1967 and 1968 from Główny Urzad Statystyczny, Statystyka Żeglugi Sródlądowej i Dróg Wodnych Sródlądowych 1968, (Warsaw: 1969), Nr. 48, Table 6, p. 4.; Data for 1969 and 1970 from the office of Żegluga na Odrze, Wrocław, July, 1971.

172

between physical output and the freight traffic can
be indicated by running a simple regression analysis
between production and the volume of traffic carried
by Żegluga na Odrze for each of the four chosen
commodities.

The author begins by examining the relationship
between coal production within the five regions under
investigation and the volume of coal traffic on the
Oder. In this case, the output of coal is referred to
as the independent variable (x) where the ton-
kilometers of coal moved is regarded as the dependent
variable (y). This decision was made on the basis of
preconceived reasoning that the demand for transportation is a derived demand. The production of coal
being located in relatively few areas and the demand
for coal being distributed throughout a wide geographic area causes this commodity to move from
points of production to points of consumption. Thus
the freight traffic of coal arises from the want of
coal by the industry or the consumer. The method of
least squares gave r^2 equal to 0.6506, meaning that
65.06 percent of the variations in the coal traffic
by the agency on the Oder is due to the variation in
the output of coal in the five regions.

Figure 6.2. shows that the line of least squares
is equal to Y = -1161153.66 + 14.26 X, showing a
relatively good fit, with r^2 equal to 65.06 percent.
This suggests that a firm relationship has existed
between the output and traffic expressed in ton-
kilometers over the period from 1957 through 1970.
Hence, one gains considerable respect for the sta-
bility embedded in Polish industrial geography in
view of the tumultuous changes in Polish industry
in the Post-World War II period.

Close inspection of the scatter diagram, however,
suggests that there may have been a slight change in
the coal traffic output relationship over this period.
The 1957 and 1958 increments in coal output were associated with somewhat higher increments in coal ton-
kilometers than was true thereafter. The point representing the year 1962 lies appreciably below the
predicted level, indicating that the output of coal
was associated with lower increments in coal ton-

FREIGHT TRAFFIC OF COAL
IN THOUSAND
TON−KILOMETERS

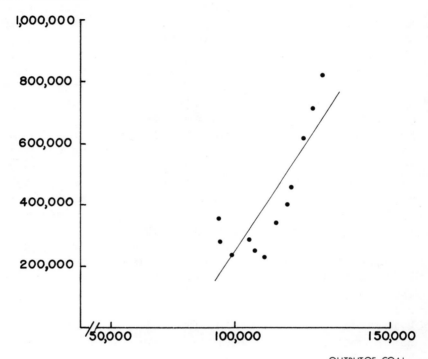

FIGURE 6.2.: CORRELATIVE RELATIONSHIP BETWEEN OUTPUT OF COAL AND
FREIGHT TRAFFIC OF COAL

Note: Negative values are not shown

174

kilometers. The observations after 1965 show that a
stable relationship has been established but it lies
at a higher level.

The largest absolute deviation between any one
year's observation from the lines occurs in 1970,
when the absolute actual coal traffic of 967,477
thousand ton-kilometers was 166,466 thousand ton-
kilometers above the 801,100 indicated by the line.
This is an error of 17.3 percent.

The steady increase in inland water coal movements, in recent years, is not particularly surprising.
In view of the continuous economic reforms in Poland
which include cost minimization and efficiency in
transportation, coal shippers apparently must think
there are substantial economic benefits in transporting their products via the Oder River. But what is
equally important is that the agency Zegluga na Odrze
in recent years became capable of meeting its demands.
This trend is reflected in Figure 6.2. which shows
that starting with 1966 the ton-kilometers of coal
moved are rising above the expected height.

The second commodity group under investigation
in this study is that of iron ore. The method of
least squares explained that 86 percent of the variation in iron ore freight traffic was attributed to the
variation in iron ore production. The equation of
the line fitted is $Y = -435056.41 + 285.68 X$. Figure
6.3. discloses a very interesting pattern of relationship between freight traffic and output in this category. For the early period, a curve concaved downward
would seem to provide the best fit. The early parallel
relationship between output and barge traffic shown
in the figure reflects the gradual depletion of the
domestic iron ore deposits in close proximity to the
Oder River and the increasing dependency of the Polish
iron and steel industry on fields not accessible by
inland waterways and Soviet iron ore shipped by railroad from the Krivoy Rog and Kerch fields to Upper
Silesia. A relatively small tonnage of high grade
Swedish iron ore continues to move by barge up the
river to the iron and steel complexes of Upper Silesia,
however, its low tonnage is inadequate to affect the
output traffic relationship. The high traffic output

FREIGHT TRAFFIC OF IRON
ORE IN THOUSAND
TON-KILOMETERS

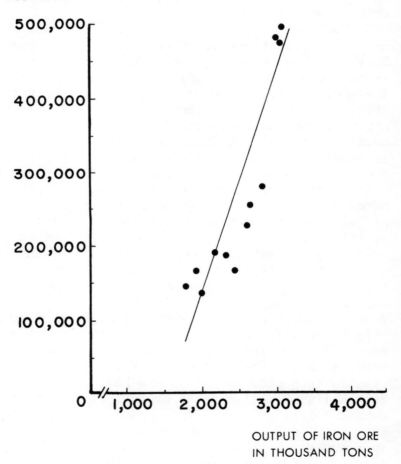

OUTPUT OF IRON ORE
IN THOUSAND TONS

FIGURE 6.3.: CORRELATIVE RELATIONSHIP BETWEEN OUTPUT OF IRON ORE AND
FREIGHT TRAFFIC OF IRON ORE

176

in 1966, 1967, and 1970 is presumed to be in response
to exploitation of newly discovered iron ore deposits
in very close proximity to the Oder River in
województwo Zielona Góra.

Turning now to the relationship between physical
volume of fertilizer production within the five
regions and inland water freight traffic carried by
Żegluga na Odrze, Figure 6.4. presents a line of regression which is equal to Y = -8390.76 + 37.78 X.
In this case the fit explained 89 percent of the
variation in fertilizer traffic on the Oder by the
variation in fertilizer production. The scatter diagram discloses a pattern significantly different than
the one for coal and iron ore for the years 1957
through 1970.

With the location of a substantial number of
chemical plants along the Oder River, the physical
output and barge freight traffic subsequently underwent substantial alteration. The establishment of
fertilizer plants in Kedzierzyn and Brzeg brought with
it a noticeable increase in the volume of fertilizer
carried by the Żegluga na Odrze. This relationship
seems to have persisted until 1967 when the fertilizer
output was associated with slightly lower barge
traffic than in the early 1960's. This decline in
tonnage of fertilizer carried by Żegluga na Odrze can
be explained perhaps in the marketing changes which
necessitate different channels of distribution. The
fertilizer produced along the Oder River in the late
1960's extends along a wider geographic market, not
necessarily accessible by the inland waterways.

Still another pattern comes to light with an
examination of the relationship between agricultural
production and agricultural commodity movement on the
Oder. In this case, the method of least squares shows
a disappointingly poor fit of 52 percent. Figure 6.5.
shows the line of least squares to be Y = -17069.15 +
1.59 X. One notes here what is evidently a graphic
indication of the fundamental changes in the late
1960's in the movement of agricultural products.
Since the conclusion of World War II and until recently, Poland was a major exporter of grain and
other agricultural products. The port of Szczecin

177

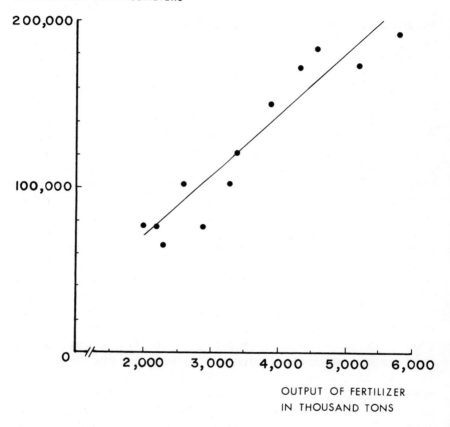

FIGURE 6.4.: CORRELATIVE RELATIONSHIP BETWEEN OUTPUT OF FERTILIZER AND
FREIGHT TRAFFIC OF FERTILIZER

Note: Negative values are not shown

FREIGHT TRAFFIC OF AGRICULTURAL PRODUCTS
IN THOUSAND TON-KILOMETERS

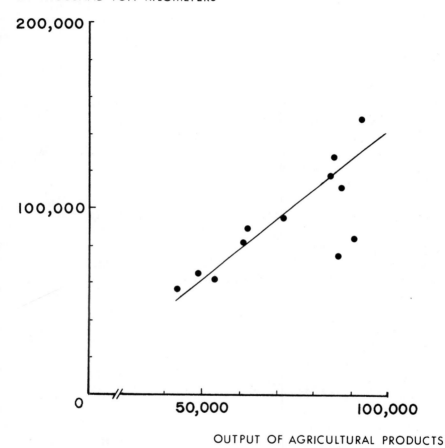

FIGURE 6.5.:   CORRELATIVE RELATIONSHIP BETWEEN OUTPUT OF AGRICULTURAL
PRODUCTS AND FREIGHT TRAFFIC OF AGRICULTURAL PRODUCTS

Note: Negative values are not shown

attained a world reputation of being the grain port of Poland. Agricultural products from the fertile Oder valley and the eastern regions moved north and northwest by inland waterways to the port of Szczecin. The seasonal demand of agricultural products for transportation and the direction of movement made the inland carriers a particularly attractive mode of transportation. In the late 1960's, however, directional changes in the movement of agricultural products occurred. Poland has ceased to be a major exporter of grain and is entering the world market with processed and manufactured goods while agricultural products are allocated for the domestic market to help feed the growing population. Agricultural products destined for the domestic market which necessitate constant break-in-bulk operations would obviously have entirely different channels of distribution.

The positive results of the above simple regression analysis gave encouragement in establishing a further relationship between the rate of industrial growth within the five województwa, Katowice, Opole, Wrocław, Zielona Góra, and Szczecin, and the rate of growth of demand for inland water transportation on the Oder. Mainly, due to the fact that in spite of these findings, the question can be asked: Can the two variables, for example, the production of coal and the freight traffic of coal, have a large degree of fit and actually be related through time without being linearly related? To eliminate this doubt, a multiple regression analysis was employed in which, aside from the two previously used variables in the simple regression analysis, the physical output of the four commodities and their freight traffic records, a third variable is introduced, the industrial index of the Gross National Product. Multiple regression analysis was used in this case, both to predict output by using freight traffic records and using the output to predict ton-kilometers. Finally, the residuals from the simple regression analysis was used in the second order of partial correlation coefficient ($r_{12.3}$) which measures the correlation between the output of each commodity and the freight

traffic independently from the industrial index of
the Gross National Product. The coefficient of correlation (r) for these set of values is equal to 0.99.
The above significant findings are summarized in the
table below.

TABLE 6.4.

DEGREE OF FIT (r^2) IN VARIOUS METHODS
OF LINEAR REGRESSION

	Coal	Iron Ore	Fertilizer	Agricultural Products	
Simple Correlation Coefficient	0.94	0.95	0.95	0.76	Using ton-km. to predict output
Adjusted for Industrial Index of GNP	0.99	0.99	0.99	0.93	Using output to predict ton-km.
Partial Correlation Coefficient Adjusted for Economic Index	0.80	0.93	0.95	0.73	

Analysis of the Oder River and Economic Development through Time

Having found a formal relationship between the growth
of industrial production and freight traffic, it would
seem instructive to investigate through time the influence of the development of industry within the five
regions and the role of the Oder River on this development. The question should be asked: How well did the
Oder serve the regions in their development? This is
an important question because inland waterways in a
socialistic economy, like in a capitalistic economy,
provide a cheap and essential transportation service
for bulk commodity, which in turn is basic for a
modern industrial economy.

In answering this particular question of how well
did the Oder River, as an artery of transportation and
the navigation agency Żegluga na Odrze, serve the five
regions, it would be useful to divide Polish experience
in navigating this waterway into periods. The examination of the performance of the Oder River as an artery
of transportation should be within the political and
economic setting of Post-World War II Poland.

181

The first period covers the years from 1946 through 1949 when the entire Polish economy underwent a drastic, fundamental structural reorganization. In the three year plan, the principle task was reconstruction of the economy from the severe war damage, in addition to carrying out political, social, and economic revolutions. War destruction of the total assets of communication and transportation facilities within the five regions under investigation were estimated by planners to be as high as 54 percent and 93 percent, respectively.[1]

The Oder waterway had been damaged during the war to the point that navigation on the river had been rendered impossible. About 1200 vessels, the remnants of the Oder fleet which had not been evacuated to the west by the retreating German Army, lay on the bottom of the channel, in the ports, and winter harbors.[2] Moreover, 45 wrecked bridges, 25 lock weirs, and other shore installations laid in ruins.[3] The reservoirs at Turawa and Otmuchów needed major repairs. In addition, there was heavy destruction in port buildings, loading facilities, and quays. For example, approximately 90 percent of the port facilities in Głogów, Malczyce, and Wrocław were devastated.

The maritime port of Szczecin, equally, the major inland water terminal, suffered greater destruction than any other port in Europe. Communications were totally paralyzed as all bridges were destroyed, the floating equipment was scuttled or taken away, port cranes were toppled into canals, and the port entrance was blocked.

The enormity of the destruction in the transportation system of the five województwa Katowice, Opole, Wrocław, Zielona Góra, and Szczecin, was a major obstacle to the recovery of these regions. There is no need to argue the point of the importance of the transportation system to the economy of the country

---

[1]
Główny Urząd Planowania Przestrzennego, Atlas Ziem Odzyskanych (Warsaw: 1947).

[2]
Z. Dziewonski, "Odra w Gospodarce Ziem Odzyskanych," Życie Gospodarcze, No. 16a (1947).

[3]
Ibid.

as it is obvious. In the first period, when the
Polish government took over this area under its administration, provision of an adequate transportation
system was of the utmost importance. For example, at
the end of the hostilities in the course of the active
campaign for settling this area by a Polish speaking
population as quickly as possible, it became evident
that the distribution and flow of the population from
the east was affected by the accessibility provided
by transportation. The areas with an inadequate
transportation system, because of the destruction,
were virtually unpopulated by Poles for several years
following the conclusion of the war. The same was
true in the case of the Oder River, transportation
was of the utmost importance, not only to the Polish
settlement of the area, but also to industry which
began to operate in Upper and Lower Silesia.

Before and during the war, local industry in the
area was heavily dependent on water carriers. In
1946, however, industry could not possibly utilize
the Oder waterway when the river and her fleet lay in
ruins. Instead, industry had to develop and depend
on alternate routes and modes of transportation.

It was recognized that in order to render the
Oder River as a useful routeway, it was necessary for
the Polish government to allocate a considerable
amount of capital. However, the commitment to the
process of rapid industrialization on the Soviet model
and the acute shortage of real capital in the period
immediately following World War II did not permit
allocation of a large number of resources to the
development of the Oder's routeway and construction
of the river fleet. Instead, the government rested
its total hopes on the railroad's ability to meet both
the qualitative and quantitative demands for movement.
In this respect the Polish National Railroad (PKP) did
its job well, in spite of the high cost per ton of
commodity moved.

Reconstruction of the Oder waterway to the prewar
level was thought by planners to be no longer sufficient to meet the anticipated demand for inland water
transportation. The general view was that a waterway
of prewar carrying capacity and technological status

183

could no longer meet the future needs of the most
industrialized area incorporated into the economic
system of Poland. The task of reconstructing and
modernizing the Oder waterway was a difficult one for
a country faced with the problems of adapting the
transportation system of these regions to the new economic direction and forces and integrating it with the
transportation system of the whole country. In view
of the enormity of the problems which Poland's economy
faced after the conclusion of the hostilities, the reconstruction and modernization of inland waterways was
not on the high priority list. This general policy
pertained not only to the Oder River, but also extended
to all inland waterways. It was a simple question of
priorities in allocating resources to the modes of
transportation and, in this case, the railroad proved
to be a more suitable and the more flexible mode of
transportation than inland waterways at that time.

In the period between 1945 and 1952 the flow of
capital and other economic resources into the development of navigation on the Oder had been held down
to a fraction of the prewar period. Judging by the
performance of the inland water carriers on the Oder,
it appears that the flow of economic resources was not
sufficient to enable this waterway and its carriers
to meet the demands imposed by the heavy and related
industries in the five województwa. As a result, a
transportation crisis on the Oder waterway developed
by 1952 which persisted through 1959. The crisis on
the Oder extended beyond its confines to the point
that the water carriers in Poland were considered
marginal by the shippers, suitable only of moving
sand and gravel at a short distance. Thus, until full
reconstruction of the Oder waterway took place and a
new modern river fleet was built, the Oder River contributed little or not at all to the economic
development of the five regions.

In spite of the shortage of real capital allocated to inland waterways, in the period prior to
1959, slow but systematic reconstruction of the Oder
waterway took place with a minimum use for the purpose of navigation. First of all, the most dangerous
damage to the water reservoirs and the embankments

184

had to be repaired as the river and the water in the reservoirs was in danger of breaking through and inundating the surrounding land. Slowly, the river was cleared of the debris of sunken boats so that by 1946 some traffic, with difficulty could move on the Oder proper and the Gliwice Canal. It was also necessary to channelize and regulate the river in some parts since under the German administration this was not completed. Construction of shore installations and a fleet were begun from scratch, for these were almost completely destroyed. In this period, two important projects were carried out, a large retention reservoir in Turów was built to help maintain the minimum depths in the channel and the new locks at Brzeg Dolny were constructed which extended the channelized portion of the Oder by 30 kilometers.

In spite of the obvious technological shortcomings of the waterway and transfer facilities, the demand for cheap transportation service in the five województwa increased monumentally. It should be pointed out that this is the same period during which Polish transportation and locational policies were directed toward holding down the demand for transportation. For example, on the completely war-devastated Oder waterway and supposedly inefficient transportation operations, freight traffic increased from 30 thousand tons in 1946 to approximately 12.9 million tons in 1952. This occurred simply because the administrative economic policies which attempted to curb the demand for transportation had been confronting powerful objective forces generating additional traffic demands within these regions. Polish industry became dispersed, dispersed in the sense that the traditional centers of industry and newly acquired centers in the western and northwestern województwa were separated by economic distance. Therefore, in view of the locational pattern of resources and population distribution, this dispersion tended to raise, for most commodities, the average length of haul. This increase of the average length of haul is barely evident in the Żegluga na Odrze shipping records but, nevertheless, it shows a trend in the rise of the average distance of commodity moved. The primary reason for the lack

of a drastic rise in the length of haul on the Oder,
until 1959, was that the railroad, at that time, was
capable of providing adequate service while water
carriers were considered marginal as a mode of transportation and poorly equipped to meet both quantitative and qualitative demands within the five
wojewodztwa.

As Table 6.5. shows, the average length of haul
on the Oder for basic commodities such as coal,
cement, and fertilizer declined rapidly to 1959.
Since 1960, when the waterway and the agency's river
fleet became fully operational and, at the same time,
when the level of service provided by the railroad on
the line Upper Silesia-Szczecin drastically declined,
one begins to see a noticeable rise in the tonnages
on the Oder and subsequently the rise in the length of
haul.

Nevertheless, the cost of transporting commodity
by water carrier on the Oder prior to full reconstruction and the adoption of push-towing in 1968, in comparison with other modes of transportation, was rather
high. Consequently, in addition to the transportation
cost factor, the emphasis on speed of industrial
development and the overall lack of locational pull
of the manufacturing establishments to the river location were fundamental factors in preventing a much
earlier development of the Oder waterway as an artery
of transportation.

As a direct consequence of the postwar selective
investment policy in transportation by the central
planning agency, an essential change was effected in
the character of the industry's methods of procure-
ment and distribution that existed in the five regions.
In a sense, it reoriented some of the basic industry,
which under the German administration heavily depended
on and was well served by the Oder waterway, into
chief dependency on the railroad for the service of
transportation.

Modernization of the Oder waterway and the subsequent rise in tonnages was primarily an adjunct to the
investment possibilities. After 1959 when the government planners showed interest in the inland waterways
and their carriers and allocated a substantial amount

TABLE 6.5.

AVERAGE HAUL PER TON OF FREIGHT ON THE ODER
(IN KILOMETERS)

Year	All Freight	Coal	Ores	Sand & Gravel	Metals and Metal Prod.	Cement	Fertilizers
1947	398	391	489	60	---	454	---
1950	409	396	475	62	---	401	385
1955	426	375	498	55	130	372	389
1957	432	382	529	50	134	375	379
1959	378	509	507	62	531	323	376
1960	467	529	538	66	451	452	406
1962	404	562	499	57	213	998	357
1964	544	605	602	60	469	717	428
1966	541	635	577	44	634	864	434
1968	537	662	611	53	637	917	456
1970	528	669	618	50	760	785	507

Sources: Główny Urząd Statystyczny, Rocznik Statystyczny Transportu 1945-1966 (Warsaw: 1967), Table 6, pp. 496-497; and Data from the office of agency "Żegluga na Odrze," Wrocław.

187

of resources to the reconstruction and modernization, one can see a gradual but persistent rise in tonnages carried by Żegluga na Odrze. By then the full activation of the Oder became important, not only to the five województwa through which the waterway flows, but to the entire economy. As a result of the accelerated development and modernization of the Oder waterway since 1968, its present structure and function within the five województwa differs from that of the pre-1959 period. The most striking difference is the increasing role that the Oder waterway is beginning to play in the locational decisions in the basic industries, such as metallurgy, chemicals, building, electric power producing and agriculture.

In assessing the relationship of the Oder River and the economic development within the study area, one can make several observations. Districts in which favorable physical and economic conditions existed for the development of heavy industry, and at the same time are contiguous to the Oder River, particularly in the województwa Katowice, Opole, and Wrocław, reached a much higher level of industrialization than the outlying districts concentrating on small or light industries as in województwa Zielona Góra and Szczecin. This disparity in industrial development among the five regions cannot be attributed to the selectivity of the Oder waterway among the industries or the inherent advantage of the inland water carriers. But rather, the differences in the level of economic development within the five regions are a response to a combination of forces such as conscious planning, accessibility, and a region's endowment in natural resources. Particularly, in view of the fact that by the time that the Oder waterway became capable of meeting the demand for the service of inland water transportation, heavy industry in Upper Silesia was not only rebuilt but had also expanded. For example, by 1959 the iron and steel industry in Upper and Lower Silesia was annually producing 2.6 million tons of pig iron and 3.9 million tons of crude steel which is 70 percent and 73 percent, respectively, of the

total Polish iron and steel production.[4] In
województwo Katowice alone, as early as 1957, 83,995
thousand tons of coal was extracted, which constituted
89.4 percent of the total Polish production.[5]

Therefore, it would be completely erroneous to
say that the Oder River prior to 1959 played a substantial role in the industrialization of these five
województwa under investigation, while it would be
quite proper to say that since 1959 the Oder River
has begun to perform a vital role in the further
industrialization of this area. With each year, not
only are the water carriers developing into highly
specialized mode of transportation but, what is more
important, the Oder River location for some industries
is becoming essential. One may speculate that with
further modernization of the routeway and the carriers'
floating equipment this mode of transportation will
be capable of providing adequate service, both
quantitatively and qualitatively, without major
interruptions. The Oder River will definitely continue
to be a major asset to the five województwa.

4

 Główny Urząd Statystyczny, Rocznik Statystyczny Przemysłu 1967 (Warsaw:
1968), Table 20, pp. 230-271.

5

 Marek Grabania, Regiony Przemysłowe Województwa Katowickiego (Katowice:
Śląski Instytut Naukowy, 1963), p. 50.

Chapter VII

Regional Development Within the Five Województwa and the Demand for Spatial Interaction

The economic development of Poland since the conclusion of World War II has led to considerable changes in the regional economic patterns and significant changes in the circulation of goods and people. If one looks at the transportation system as the means by which circulation takes place, or to be more specific as a vital link between spatially distributed points, such as location of raw materials, industry, and markets, then the volume and the pattern of transportation required by the economy would clearly depend, aside from the type of economic activity, on the location and locational relationship of raw materials, place of production, and the points of consumption. If these places of economic activity can be related from transportation's point of view as focal points, then any change in the location of one of these focal points would tend to alter the entire relationship between all of these points, necessitating changes in the links, thus change in the pattern.

The Oder River as a link within the inland water transportation system, due to physical limitation in the directional flow of the river, does not change its direction in response to the desired direction of movement. Hence, there have been significant changes in the Oder's hinterland since being incorporated into the rest of Poland. The river as a link assumed a new function in the relationship of the distribution of raw materials, centers of production, and markets. In view of these assumed changes, an analysis of the commodity flow patterns in response to regional changes must be made.

190

The analysis of the average distance of freight movement alone will not be sufficient to detect changes in the function of the Oder within its hinterland because they are made up of overlapping long, medium, and short-distance hauls. They conceal the essential characteristics which typifies the circulation of goods. In analyzing the response of the modes of transportation to changes in the regional patterns, aside from the analysis of distance, one should consider the intraregional and interregional commodity flow, the location of the Oder as an artery of transportation in relation to source of raw materials, centers of production, and markets.

In this chapter, a brief study of the response of the Oder to the changing regional patterns is made. The analysis also involves the examination of intraregional and interregional flow of the four commodities on the Oder which constituted, in 1970, approximately 90 percent of the tonnage carried by the agency, Żegluga na Odrze.

General Economic Impact of the Oder River

The most effective way to determine the economic effects of the Oder River navigation would be to trace through on a commodity basis. One danger of such an approach is that the total impact is submerged in the analysis of specific industries. The aggregate impact can be traced by looking at the region's effects of the river as a whole. Nevertheless, commodity analysis shows that Polish industry is making a subtle but pronounced movement to the river's banks. In the Oder valley the boom is only in its infancy. Cheap electric power, an important locational magnet, has barely had time to make itself felt in the postwar period. In addition, the development of huge industrial complexes such as the aluminum industry and metal-alloy plants is a harbinger of what hydro- and thermoelectric plants located along the river will mean in the future. This coupled with the steel complexes in Szczecin and the nonferrous metals in Iwiny, Legnica, and Wilków, and the petroleum refineries add up to an imposing array of basic industries in the Oder valley. Chemical plants such as Odra cement

191

works in Opole, the nitrogen works in Kedzierzyn, Rokita organic chemical works in Brzeg, Wizów chemical works in Gorzów, and the staple fiber and rayon works in Jelemia Góra and Szczecin show preference for a river location. Of course, these primary industries all attract complementary manufacturing and this secondary wave of growth has already started. For example, the electrical appliance industry in the city of Wrocław in recent years has greatly expanded. This central location allows the plants to receive large volumes of metals by water carrier from upriver and simultaneously enjoy low outbound transportation costs by rail.

Clearly, in the spirit of operating the Polish economy more efficiently, the shift of industry within the Oder valley to the river is destined to continue. All the attractions of the waterway that have developed in recent years remain and the industrial boom along the river will have a tendency of breeding a secondary boom of its own creation.

One indication of the size of the industrial boom occurring in the valley is the amount of capital invested in new plants and equipment and in the expansion of the existing plants. Unfortunately, the statistical data showing annual investment outlay in new plants and equipment which would support the above speculation was not available to the author. In relative terms, it is quite apparent in the five województwa, Katowice, Opole, Wrocław, Zielona Góra, and Szczecin, the investments made in industry, per inhabitant, are higher than in the remaining twelve województwa of the country.[1] The same result can be achieved by looking at the sheer number of manufacturing establishments and the rise in industrial employment.

Table 7.1. indicates that in 1960, of the total manufacturing establishments, 42.4 percent were located in the five województwa, Katowice, Opole, Wrocław, Zielona Góra, and Szczecin, while the

[1] Based on the author's personal field observation during travel in the area, May to August, 1966, 1968, and 1971.

TABLE 7.1.

COMPARISON OF MANUFACTURING AND INDUSTRIAL EMPLOYMENT IN THE STUDY
AREA WITH THE REST OF POLAND (FOR SELECTED YEARS)

	Within Five Województwa Under Investigation			Rest of Poland		
	1955	1960	1970	1955	1960	1970
No. of Manufacturing Establishments	- - -	12,137	37,763	- - -	28,631	78,927
Employment in Industry in Thousands	1186.8	1200.1	1514.3	1492.2	1697.2	2274.4
Employment in Industry as % of Total Employment	50.3%	46.0%	49.3%	37.1%	36.1%	38.9%

Sources: Główny Urząd Statystyczny, Rocznik Statystyczny Przemysłu 1945-1966 (Warsaw: 1967); Główny Urząd Statystyczny, Rocznik Statystyczny 1971 (Warsaw: 1971).

remaining twelve województwa in Poland shared 57.6 percent of the manufacturing establishments. The data for 1970 indicates a more favorable percentage distribution of manufacturing establishments for the województwa within the study area. The five regions under investigation in 1970 contained 47.8 percent of all manufacturing establishments. However, if one looks only at the numerical distribution of the manufacturing establishments as the sole indicator of the region's economic contribution to the nation's economic strength, one would invariably get a distorted picture. Not only do the manufacturing establishments vary in size, ranging from gigantic steel foundaries employing thousands of skilled workers to small ceramic "factories" employing a few artisans, but they also differ in their importance to the economy.

Therefore, one of the major indicators of the region's level of industrial development or its contribution to the total economy would be the ratio of employment in industry to the total employment, or the region's share of industrial employment in relation to the rest of the country. For example, in 1955 the five województwa contiguous to the Oder River contained 79.5 percent of the total employed in industry. In 1960 and 1970 their relative share dropped to 70.7 percent and 66.6 percent, respectively. In the ratio of industrial employment to the total employment within the regions, one can see that in 1955 in the five województwa under study 50.3 percent of the total employment was in industry while in the rest of the country the percentage was significantly lower, only 37.1 percent. In 1970, industrial employment in the study area declined slightly to 49.3 percent, while rising in the remaining województwa to 38.9 percent.

Taking both the number of manufacturing establishments and employment in industry as an indication of the level of industrialization, it can be seen that in the five regions contiguous to the Oder River, the number of manufacturing establishments rose 67.9 percent from 1960 to 1970, while the number of manufacturing establishments in the remaining regions of Poland increased 63.7 percent. The percentage change in the industrial employment for the same period shows that in the five regions employment in industry rose by 20.8 percent, while in the remaining regions of the country the increase was slightly higher, increasing by 26.4 percent. Nevertheless, major disproportions continue to exist between the western regions of the country and the central and eastern regions, between the old industrial agglomerations and the slowly developing new centers.

Analysis of the data in the table above indicates two trends. First, it is quite evident by the distribution of the industrial employment that Polish industry in the past fifteen years has been gradually decentralizing in favor of the previously poorly industrialized regions. Nevertheless, the distribution of natural resources and locational inertia created by the traditional centers of industry continue to act as an important magnet in attracting new industry to the already well-established centers. The fact is that, contrary to the wishes of the central planning agency, the bulk of Polish industry is located in the south-western regions of the country and the five województwa in the Oder River basin contain a major share.

Second, the gradual changing economic structure of the country is manifested in the percentage of employment in industry to the total employment. In spite of the fact that industrial employment declined slightly in the 1955 to 1970 period, the rise in subsequent years indicates that Poland is becoming an industrial economy. The decline in industrial employment in 1960, after a period of forceful industrialization effort, denotes a certain degree of relaxation and subsequent allocation of resources, including labor, to other segments of the economy. A rise again in 1970 in industrial employment seems to be a response to economic forces rather than political.

What is apparent from the analysis of the data is that the Oder River basin continues to be an area of high industrial concentration. If one compares individual województwa within the study area with the rest of the country, the findings are even more favorable.

If one takes as a base, not the absolute increases in industrial employment but, the rise in

195

industrial employment in relation to the physical size of the region, this would throw a light on the changes in the density of industrial employment. For example, it can be seen that in the period of 1947 to 1959 Katowice shows the highest increase of industrial employment per 100 square kilometers, an increase of 3,467, followed by Wrocław with 880 and Opole with 837.[2] This absolute increase in industrial employment can be compared with województwa Warszawa and Lublin, having 641 and 202 employees per 100 square kilometers, respectively.[3] The rise in industrial employment in relationship to the size of the area was the slowest in the województwa that are designated by the planners as developing or underdeveloped and was the highest in the traditional area of large industrial agglomeration. The primary obstacle to decentralization, thus more even distribution of industry throughout the country and comprehensive economic development of primarily agricultural regions, was the early emphasis on the speed of industrialization. In the 1950's, sheer output was a measure of success or failure of the economy under the quota system. Consequently, already established centers of industry received heavy outlays of capital. This only further aggravated regional differences. A more even distribution of industry throughout the country was obtainable only at the price of weakening the already established heavy industry in Upper and Lower Silesia, thus lowering the level of the Gross National Product. This price was thought to be too much for the young country to bear.

In the period 1959 to 1970 one can see a more selective diversification of Polish industry. An attempt is being made to integrate clusters of industry in incorporated territories in the west with the rest of the nation's economy. Corollary to the development and expansion of both the already established and the newly developing centers of industry

[2]
Tadeusz Mrzygłód, Politica Rozmieszczenia Przemysłu w Polsce 1946-1980 (Warsaw: Ksiażka i Wiedza, 1962), p. 58.

[3]
Ibid.

is the unification of these into a gigantic urban-industrial agglomerations. For example, the Silesian-Kraków industrial region lying at the eastern extremity of the Gliwice Canal, at the end of 1970, employed approximately 32 percent of the nation's total industrial labor force. Another sizable industrial agglomeration within the Oder River basin is the Wałbrzych industrial region in województwo Wrocław, which in 1970 employed approximately 13 percent of the nation's industrial workers.

Several smaller important clusters of industry are located along the Oder, stretching from Koźle in the województwo Opole to the city of Wrocław. The middle section of the Oder valley, which lies within the województwa Zielona Góra and the southern portions of Szczecin, is considered to be poorly developed as it has the least number of industrial establishments and its industrial employment is slightly below the national average. Nevertheless, what little industry exists in these two regions and what is being presently established show a preference for a river location. Northern Szczecin, which includes the maritime port by the same name, has an important cluster of heavy industry ranging from iron and steel plants to thermoelectric power plants, all of which have a river location.

In summary, the Oder River basin is characterized by relatively wide extremes in economic development. It has localities among the highest per capita share of industrial output and some areas with very low per capita industrial output. It has an extraordinary wide diversification in its economic development, including every major type of economic activity in Poland. In this respect, it is one of the most balanced economic regions of the country. Population settlements, mining, manufacturing, agriculture, and forestry are all concentrated along the Oder River. The period, from 1959 to the present but particularly since 1968, is marked by rapid modernization of the waterway and the agency's floating equipment. The subsequent rise in the tonnages carried by the Żegluga na Odrze is indicative of the relationship between the technological capabilities of the waterway and the

FIGURE 7.1.:   1938 COMMODITY FLOW ON THE ODER RIVER

TABLE 7.2.

TONNAGE AND THE DIRECTION OF COMMODITY MOVEMENT
(IN THOUSAND TONS)

Place	1910 Up River	1910 Down River	1938 Up River	1938 Down River	1947 Up River	1947 Down River	1970 Up River	1970 Down River
Gliwice	--	--	--	--	90	450	137	520
Kozle	638	2735	470	3201	320	500	640	914
Wroclaw	1070	2831	787	3595	410	968	870	1351
Glogow	1144	3210	--	--	--	--	--	--
Prybrzeg	1185	3331	1055	4119	485	940	921	1459
Kostrzyn	1041	1503	991	1544	480	885	871	1438
Szczecin	2062	1323	2443	1814	450	862	1019	1415
Swinoujscie	--	--	420	809	--	428	--	600

Sources: Nils Holmberg, Oderhndeln (Lund: 1941); Engineer Research Office, Navigable Waterways of Germany (Strategic Intelligence Branch, Military Intelligence Division, VIII), August, 1944; Statistics for 1947 and 1970 from the records of the agency Żegluga na Odrze, Wrocław, 1971.

199

role that it plays in facilitating industrial development within the five województwa.

Changing Regional Patterns and the Oder River

Prior to World War II, the directional flow of commodity in the study area did not correspond with the
longitudinal axis of the Oder River but, rather, it
deviated westward toward Greater Berlin from the
general north-south direction. If one looks at Table
7.2. in conjunction with Figure 7.1., which shows the
commodity flow on the Oder River in 1938, one can say
that the intensity and the tonnages carried on individual sectors of the river corresponded to the physical conditions on the river. The tonnages, like the
depths in the navigable channel, rose with the northerly
direction and both drastically declined in the middle
sector of the Oder River. Both the intensity of
commodity flow and the depths in the navigable channel
rose again in the lower sector from Cedynia to
Szczecin. It should be pointed out, however, that the
intensity of flow was not predetermined by the physical
conditions of the individual sectors of the waterway
but, rather, the lack of use of a particular sector of
the Oder River contributed to its physical deficiency
by administrative neglect.

Upper Silesia, an important producer of raw
materials and industrial output, had a sizable northerly outflow of commodity by the inland waterway.
In Koźle, for example, in 1938 the annual flow of
freight down the Oder was 3.2 million tons, at Wrocław
the tonnages increased to 4.0 million.[4] In Przybrzeg
this northerly commodity flow, approximately 3 million
tons, was diverted to the west through the Oder-Spree
Canal in the direction of Greater Berlin.[5] In the
middle Oder from Przybrzeg to Cedynia, the least suitable portion of the Oder for navigation, the gains of
400 thousand tons from the local ports in this section
could hardly balance the significant loss in freight

[4]
Gerhard Giesecke, Oderschiffahrts und Oder Wirtsdiaftsfrzgen (Emsdetten:
1940), pp. 41-46.

[5]
Ibid.

200

which was diverted westward. From the east by the
tributaries, the Warta and the Noteć, the Oder received 240 thousand tons of freight while, at this
point, it diverted to the easterly flow 73 thousand
tons.[6] The attraction of Berlin and the provinces
lying west of the Oder was of such a magnitude that,
in the vicinity of Kostrzyń, the commodity flow moving
down the Oder toward the maritime port of Szczecin was
merely 1700 thousand tons.[7] A portion of this tonnage
at Cedynia, at the point where the Oder is linked with
the Hohenzollern Canal, here too was directed toward
the west. Cedynia was a point of convergence for
commodity moving eastward from the general direction
of Greater Berlin and the western regions through the
Hozenzollern Canal and commodity moving north via the
Oder River. In total, these two flows equalled
approximately 800 thousand tons at Cedynia, half of
which was unloaded in the small ports lying down the
river, leaving approximately 400 thousand tons to
eventually reach the port of Szczecin.

If one looks at the commodity flow up the Oder
River, one may notice certain structural similarities
in both flows. As in the case of the freight movement
down the river, in the up-river flow the primary
direction of the flow was toward Berlin. These two
commodity flows from the southeast and northeast converged on the area of Greater Berlin. For example,
in 1938, 2443 thousand tons of freight moved southward
from Szczecin, while at Cedynia 1500 thousand tons of
it was diverted in a westward direction through the
Hozenzollern Canal.[8] Thus the middle portion of the
Oder, north of Cedynia, receives less than a million
tons of freight, from which one should subtract 130
thousand tons which moved east through the Oder
tributaries, the Warta and the Notec. Therefore,
south of Kostrzyn, the total southward flow of freight

[6]
Ibid.

[7]
Ibid.

[8]
Engineer Research Office, VIII, pp. 429-431.

was only 884 thousand tons. The small port of
Przybrzeg was the point where the flow of approximately 300 thousand tons moving on the Oder-Spree
Canal, from the direction of the Greater Berlin area,
met the southward movement on the Oder proper. At
that point, the commodity flow destined for Silesia
was slightly over 1 million tons. As the flow moved
up the river, tonnages gradually declined along the
way and the flow value of not quite one-half million
tons reached the southern terminal port of Koźle.

As one can see, the general direction of commodity flow on the Oder in 1938 was under the great
influence of Berlin and its vicinity. The mastery of
Berlin as a point of destination can be illustrated
by pointing to the aggregate and directional movement
of freight. For example, from the extreme south-
eastern portion of Germany, almost 3 million tons of
freight moved toward Berlin and the western provinces.
Outflow of freight from Upper and Lower Silesia to the
west via inland waterways was two and one-half times
larger than the return flow down the river. From
Szczecin and Western Pomerania more than 1.5 million
tons was moved westward.[9] In the return flow eastward, from Greater Berlin and the western provinces
through the inland waterway connecting the Elbe with
the Oder, significantly smaller tonnages were moved.
In total, Greater Berlin and the western provinces
of Germany received 4.5 million tons of freight from
Silesia and Szczecin, in the form of raw materials,
manufactured goods, and agricultural products and,
in return, the west assigned slightly over 1 million
tons for destinations in the east.[10]

It is interesting to note that there was more of
a balanced relationship in the movement of commodity
on the Oder River itself, between the upper and lower
Oder valley. For example, the port of Szczecin received from Upper Silesia 568 thousand tons of freight
and consigned to Upper Silesia 375 thousand tons.[11]

[9]
Ibid.
[10]
Ibid., pp. 437-442.
[11]
Ibid.

202

From Lower Silesia, Szczecin received 224 thousand
tons and was sending up river 369 thousand tons.[12]
Together, Szczecin received from Upper and Lower
Silesia 693 thousand tons and consigned for shipment
to Silesia 643 thousand tons.[13]

The movement of commodity on the Oder from the
end of the nineteenth century until the outbreak of
World War I rose rapidly. For example, the tonnages
carried on the Oder, at Wrocław, was 1.8 million tons
in 1880, increasing to 2 million and 5.5 million in
1910 and 1913, respectively.[14] After World War I,
the total tonnages on the Oder fell rapidly, largely
due to the new economic directions arising from the
political partition of Silesia. While a large portion of Upper Silesia was awarded to Poland, it was
soon excluded from economic use of the Oder River.
However, after Hitler came into power in 1933, in
spite of the small German holdings of Silesia, tonnages on the Oder rose gradually until the outbreak
of World War II. This rise in tonnages was a result
of the forward German thrust in the preparations for
war. Nevertheless, none of the pre-war years surpassed
more than 80 percent of the 1913 tonnages.

As one can see from Table 7.2. and by comparing
Figures 7.1. and 7.2., the freight flow intensity and
general direction is not much different between the
years 1910 and 1938. In both cases the commodity flow
from southeast and northeast converged on Berlin. The
only significant difference is the intensity of the
flow on the Oder's tributaries, the Warta and Noteć,
linking the Oder River with the lower reaches of the
Vistula. In 1910, when both of these tributaries were
under Prussian administration, sizable tonnages were
exchanged by inland waterways between East Prussia and
the western part of the state. Later, however, in
1938 when political boundaries had cut across the east-
west flowing streams, very little traffic, either
German or Polish, moved on the Warta, Noteć, and the

[12]
  Ibid.
[13]
  Ibid.
[14]
  Ibid.

lower Vistula. In this respect, the political boundary between Poland and Germany was such a significant barrier that even great economic incentives to trade were unable to overcome it.

The fundamental changes in regional structure and the pattern of movement of commodity on the Oder was forced on the Polish planners and, at the same time, fostered by them. The examination of Figures 7.3. and 7.4. reveal that the Pre-World War II pattern has been modified to the point of nonrecognition by the changes in the direction and intensity of flow. The total freight traffic on the Oder in 1970, in comparison, is only a fraction of the German traffic. It constitutes approximately 74 percent of the total 1938 tonnages. What is more important in the analysis of the function of the waterway are not the total tonnages, but the traffic flow intensity on the individual sectors and the direction of movement between the points of origin and destination. The shift in the political boundaries to the west of the Oder River in the south shattered the ascendancy of Berlin on this waterway. Unlike the Pre-World War II pattern of flow, the highest flow intensity presently is between Upper Silesia and the port of Szczecin, thus along the longitudinal axis of the Oder River. By these fundamental changes, the Oder River became, in the true sense of the word, a major artery of transportation along its entire length. In turn, this development necessitates navigational improvements of the middle sector of the river neglected by the Germans.

Examination of the data in Table 7.2. which shows the commodity flow at various points along the waterway for different periods, indicates that in the middle part of the Oder there is a great deal of similarity in the flows in 1938 and 1970. In the regional distribution of traffic requirement and traffic flow, both in 1947 and 1970, as indicated by the statistics in Table 7.2., there is a greater degree of complementarity between Silesia and the maritime port of Szczecin than was true in the 1938 period. One would also expect that in the near future, with the modernization of the Oder tributaries,

FIGURE 7.2.:   1910 COMMODITY FLOW ON THE ODER RIVER

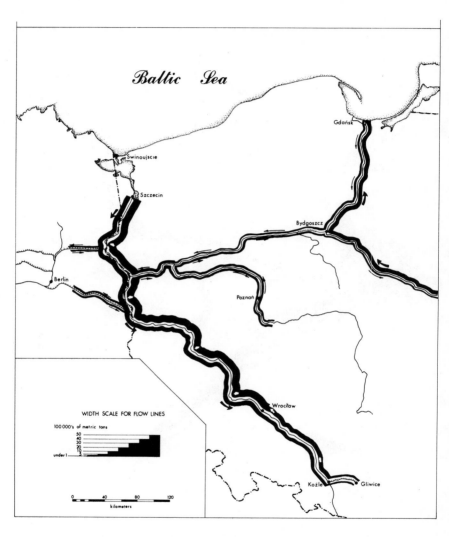

FIGURE 7.3.: 1970 COMMODITY FLOW ON THE ODER RIVER

206

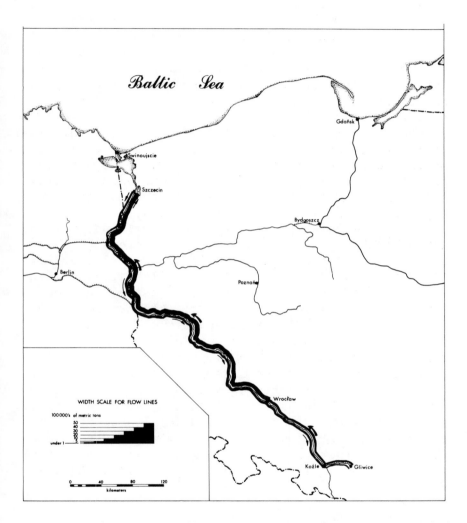

FIGURE 7.4.:   1947 COMMODITY FLOW ON THE ODER RIVER

207

the Warta and the Noteć, these will show an increase
in tonnages carried. The development of the port
facilities at Wocławek is one example of an attempt
to expand the movement of inland water traffic on
these two tributaries.

It would seem fair to conclude that traffic
growth on the Oder has resulted in the strengthening
of the hinterland's concentration. In addition, to
some extent, traffic growth and commodity diversification resulted in functional changes in the river's
hinterland. Both the shape and intensity of a
hinterland vary with changes in the direction and
volume of commodity flows at different points of time.
In the Post-World War II period, the major influence
on the Oder River hinterland has been the growth in
the volume of established commodity movements, parallel with the directional change of movement as have
occurred in the last twenty-four years.

The expansion of the iron and steel industry in
Upper Silesia had a paramount influence on the intensification of inward commodity flows. In similar
fashion, outward moving coal from Silesia, as a point
of origin, to the new centers of industry, has become
more significant in recent years. At the same time,
an internal diversification and dispersion has
occurred in the chemical and building material industries and, in recent years, these have shown a
preference for the river location.

The present traffic on the Oder is dominated by
raw materials such as coal, iron ore, sand and gravel,
and to a lesser extent by agricultural products, and
the direction of flow is heavily imbalanced toward
the north. Therefore, it is highly desirable to take
a closer look at the intraregional and interregional
flow of these individual commodities.

Geography of Commodity Transport
The analysis of major commodity traffic on the Oder
is somewhat limited by the incomplete release of
data by the Polish statistical office. In spite of
this difficulty, even a limited review of broad
traffic trends can provide one with a skeletal
insight into one aspect of the regional development

208

and industrialization process. Therefore, in this
section an analysis is undertaken concerning interregional movement, by the Oder waterway, of bulk
commodity such as coal, sand and gravel, iron ore,
and agricultural products. The available statistical
data on the shipment of raw materials in 1970 indicates that the entire supply of coal for export and
industries located in the Oder River valley comes from
Upper and Lower Silesia. Thus the shipment of coal
is northward to Wrocław and Szczecin and to the other
smelting and power producing plants located along
the river's course.

In spite of the persistent effort of the Polish
planners to decentralize the Polish iron and steel
industry throughout the years, there have been no
significant changes in the flow of coal. The coal
supplied to the western województwa comes entirely
from Katowice, Opole, and the Wałbrzych area in
województwo Wrocław. Coal still moves north and
northwest from the outlying regions in the south to
the manufacturing centers of Poland. The present
geographic pattern of interregional and intraregional
coal shipments within the study area can be examined
in the table below.

Examination of Table 7.3. along with Figure 7.3.,
which graphically presents the interregional distribution of coal, indicates that the largest consigner
of coal shipped by inland water carriers is województwo
Katowice, with 61.0 percent of the total coal tonnage
shipped via the Oder River. This region is followed
by województwo Wrocław and Opole with 18.4 and 15.5
percent, respectively. In total, these three regions
account for 95.0 percent of the coal tonnage consigned
for shipment via this inland waterway. In turn, the
largest single receiver of coal is województwo Szczecin
with 20.5 percent of the total tonnage of coal carried
on the Oder. It is interesting to note that the
entire consignment of coal via inland waterways from
the coal producing regions is destined for shipment
outside the region of origin. In the województwa
Katowice, Opole, and Wrocław, intraregional distribution of coal does not take place by water carrier,
whereas in województwo Szczecin, the largest receiver

TABLE 7.3.

INTERREGIONAL EXCHANGE OF COAL VIA ODER WATERWAY IN 1970 (IN TONS)

Origin \ Destination	Total	Katowice	Opole	Szczecin	Wrocław	Zielona Góra
Katowice	967,137	---	21,286	100,725	117,718	----
Opole	245,372	---	---	148,986	14,299	----
Szczecin	78,058	---	---	53,564	---	----
Wrocław	292,375	---	---	22,582	---	----
Zielona Góra	---	---	---	---	---	----
TOTAL	1,582,942					

Source: Główny Urząd Statystyczny, Przewozy Ładunków Żegluga Śródlądową Pomiędzy Województwami i Wojewódzkie Bilanse Przewozów Ładunków 1966-1970 Nr. 92 (Warsaw: July, 1971).

210

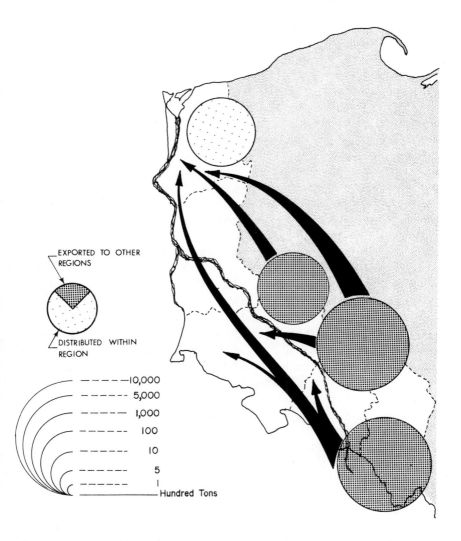

EXPORTED TO OTHER
REGIONS

DISTRIBUTED WITHIN
REGION

10,000
5,000
1,000
100
10
5
1
Hundred Tons

FIGURE 7.5.:   INTERREGIONAL DISTRIBUTION OF COAL BY THE ODER WATERWAY

211

of coal, the entire internal distribution within this region takes place by water carriers.

The primary explanation for these differences in the interregional distribution of coal lies in the variations in the accessibility of different modes of transportation, directional movement, and the channels of distribution. For example, coal from Upper Silesia moves a relatively short distance by rail east and southeast of the Gliwice Canal to the iron and steel plants in "Górnoślaski Okreg Przemysłowy" which is also accessible to the inland water carriers.[15] Nevertheless, the intraregional distribution of coal in województwo Katowice, due to short distances, direction of movement, and accessibility, is done entirely by rail. On the other hand, the coal consigned for shipment to distant outlying regions north and northwest whenever possible is transported by inland water carriers as the cheaper mode of transportation. In województwo Szczecin, due to the river location of iron and steel plants and power producing plants, the reconsignment of coal from storage yards within the region takes place by inland water carriers even when involving relatively short distances.

Unlike coal, the interregional movement of iron ore by inland waterways is less significant. This stems from the fact that the deposits of this natural resource have been exhausted in close proximity to the river location. Consequently, the Polish iron and steel industry largely depends on domestic and foreign iron ore shipped by rail. Table 7.4. shows the interregional shipment of iron ore via the Oder River.

The table shows that three regions, Szczecin, Zielona Góra, and Worcław are the sole consigners of iron ore for shipment by the agency Żegluga na Odrze. The major single consigner of iron ore to be shipped by the Oder is województwo Szczecin, 59.5 percent of its total consignment moves to województwo Katowice. The entire inland water consignment of the newly discovered iron ore fields in Zielona Góra moves south

<hr>

[15] Górnośląski Okręg Przemysłowy (Upper Silesian Industrial Region).

TABLE 7.4.

INTERREGIONAL EXCHANGE OF IRON ORE VIA ODER WATERWAY IN 1970   (IN TONS)

Origin \ Destination	Total	Katowice	Opole	Szczecin	Wrocław	Zielona Góra
Katowice	---	---	---	---	---	---
Opole	---	---	---	---	---	---
Szczecin	25,215	15,000	---	10,215	---	---
Wrocław	1,791	1,791	---	---	---	---
Zielona Góra	12,673	12,673	---	---	---	---
TOTAL	39,679					

Source: Główny Urząd Statystyczny, Przewozy Ładunków Żeglugą Śródlądową Pomiędzy Województwami i Wojewódzkie Bilanse Przewozów Ładunków 1966-1970 Nr. 92 (Warsaw: July, 1971)

to Upper Silesia. Analyzing the table with Figure
7.6. which presents interregional distribution of
iron ore, shows that the directional movement of iron
ore is opposite to that of coal.

Sand and gravel movement, the second largest
tonnage on the Oder waterway, is somewhat more complicated. In order for a load of sand and gravel to
be recorded as part of the Oder's tonnages, it must
travel a minimum distance of five kilometers. Sand
and gravel acquired from dregging operations performed
by "Zarzad Wodny" is counted as part of the tonnage
carried by Żegluga na Odrze if the movement extends
over the minimum limit of five kilometers.

The general abundance of sand and gravel in the
post-glacial topography of the area and the extremely
low cost per ton has a pronounced effect on the interregional distribution. In other words, sand and
gravel is not transportable over long distance.
Table 7.5. shows that out of 1,482,273 tons of sand
and gravel carried by the agency Żegluga na Odrze,
89.4 percent is distributed within the region of
consignment.

The single largest shipper of sand and gravel
by inland water carrier is województwo Szczecin with
58.8 percent of the total tonnage, followed closely
by województwo Wrocław with 31.3 percent. Thus these
two regions make up 90.1 percent of the total sand and
gravel tonnage carried by the agency Żegluga na Odrze.

In the interregional movement of sand and gravel,
as can be seen in Table 7.5., the only major shipper
of that commodity is województwo Opole, 88.6 percent
of its 146,142 ton consignment is shipped to
województwo Katowice. The only other region shipping
sand and gravel outside the confines of its boundaries
is województwo Szczecin.

The flow and the pattern of movement can be seen
in Figure 7.7., which surprisingly shows that some
sand and gravel from Szczecin travels the considerable
distance to województwa Opole and Katowice. This
small tonnage, which can be considered a nontransfer-
rable commodity over long distances, is part of the
load on the return movement of empty coal hoppers up
the river.

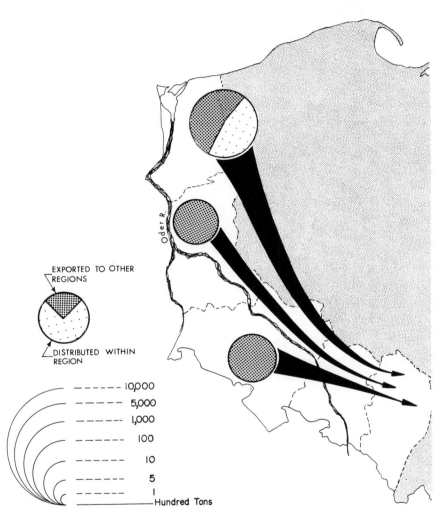

FIGURE 7.6.: INTERREGIONAL DISTRIBUTION OF IRON ORE BY THE ODER
WATERWAY

TABLE 7.5.

INTERREGIONAL EXCHANGE OF SAND AND GRAVEL VIA ODER IN 1970 (IN TONS)

Origin \ Destination	Total	Katowice	Opole	Szczecin	Wrocław	Zielona Góra
Katowice	---	---	---	---	---	---
Opole	146,142	129,590	16,552	---	---	---
Szczecin	871,654	21,468	5,795	844,391	---	---
Wrocław	464,477	---	---	---	464,477	---
Zielona Góra	---	---	---	---	---	---
TOTAL	1,482,273					

Source: Główny Urząd Statystyczny, Przewozy Ładunków Żegluga Sródlądową Pomiędzy Województwami i Wojewódzkie Bilanse Przewozów Ładunków 1966-1970 Nr. 92 (Warsaw: July, 1971).

216

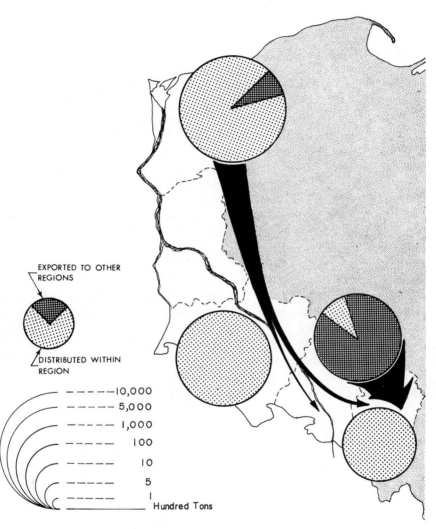

EXPORTED TO OTHER
REGIONS

DISTRIBUTED WITHIN
REGION

————————10,000
————— 5,000
————— 1,000
————— 100
————— 10
————— 5
————— 1
Hundred Tons

FIGURE 7.7.:   INTERREGIONAL DISTRIBUTION OF SAND AND GRAVEL BY THE
ODER WATERWAY

217

The interregional traffic of agricultural products in this traditionally agricultural country has
always been small. It stems from the fact that most
województwa, to a large extent, are still self-
sufficient. The regional specialization which is
developing in Poland is not exclusive to the point
where a województwa with industrial agglomerations
would not have, at the same time, a large segment of
its population engaged in agriculture.

As one can see in Table 7.6., the interregional
shipment of agricultural commodity via the Oder River
is virtually nonexistent. Out of 30,913 tons of
agricultural products carried by the agency Żegluga
na Odrze in 1970 only 2.8 percent was counted as the
interregional movement.

The largest single shipper of agricultural products via the Oder River within the five regions, as
is shown in Figure 7.8. is województwo Szczecin, with
93.7 percent of the total movement, followed by
województwo Opole with 5.9 percent. The only other
region to record shipment in 1970 of agricultural
products by water carrier was województwo Wrocław.
This movement primarily consisted of shipment of sugar
beets, as in the case of Szczecin and Opole, to the
local refineries located along the banks of the Oder.

The examination of the intraregional and interregional movement of the four commodities within the
five regions under investigation permits one to make
the generalization that the distribution or mal-
distribution of inputs of production with respect to
each other, is permanently embedded in the area's
economic environment. Consequently, a policy intended
to reduce the traffic-output ratio confronts a massive
barrier. Therefore, with the expected rise in quantitative demand for transportation, one would also
expect a rise in qualitative demand necessitating
greater specialization among carriers.

TABLE 7.6.

INTERREGIONAL EXCHANGE OF AGRICULTURAL PRODUCTS VIA ODER IN 1970   (IN TONS)

Origin \ Destination	Total	Katowice	Opole	Szczecin	Wrocław	Zielona Góra
Katowice	---	---	---	---	---	---
Opole	1,834	---	1,834	---	---	---
Szczecin	28,972	---	234	23,398	860	---
Wrocław	---	---	---	---	107	---
Zielona Góra	---	---	---	---	---	---
TOTAL	30,913					

Source: Główny Urząd Statystyczny, Przewozy Ładunków Żegluga Śródlądową Pomiędzy Województwami i Wojewódzkie Bilanse Przewozów Ladunkow 1966-1970 Nr. 92 (Warsaw: July, 1971)

219

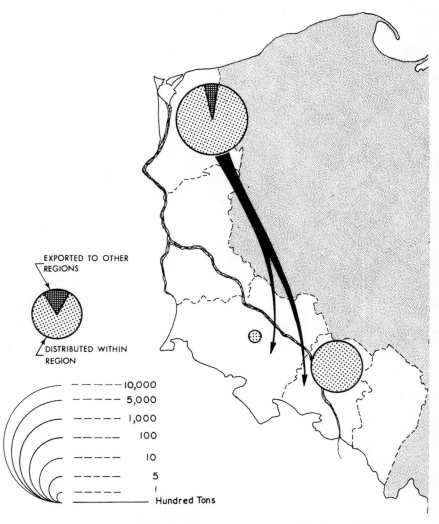

FIGURE 7.8.: INTERREGIONAL DISTRIBUTION OF AGRICULTURAL PRODUCTS
BY THE ODER WATERWAY

Chapter VIII
Conclusion

An analysis of the Oder River, as an artery of transportation and its role in the economic development
within the five województwa, indicates that the
waterway in the period immediately following the
conclusion of World War II has responded rather
sluggishly to the demands imposed by the economy.
The importance of local natural resources to the
economic growth of the five regions under investigation is most pronounced. The major identifiable
characteristics of the economy of these regions is
that they are centers of mining and heavy industry.
The development of the natural resources within the
area such as bituminous coal, lignite, copper, lead,
and zinc, and large outlays of capital in the
development of heavy and related industries created
immense quantitative and qualitative demands for the
service of transportation. Therefore, investment in
the system of transportation has been essential to
the exploitation of natural resources and the development of industry within the area. In view of the
limited economic resources at the disposal of the
planners in the Post-World War II period, the
principal investment, understandably, was not in the
inland waterways but, rather, in the higher cost but
more flexible mode, the railroad.

At the present time, the Oder River is mainly
an artery of transportation of internal significance
which serves the economy as a major link between
Silesia and the maritime port of Szczecin. The state
agency navigating the waterway, Żegluga na Odrze, is
the most prominent water carrier, not only the Oder
River itself, but also in the nation as a whole. The

221

Oder River as an international waterway, in comparison, has very little importance. The international exchange of commodities via inland waterways with Poland amounts to only several thousand tons annually, while only 10 percent of all transit through Poland avails itself of this water carrier. It should be pointed out that before the Oder River would be able to play a more eminent role in the nation's transportation system there is a need for additional modernization of the waterway.

The full development of the Oder as an artery of transportation should be associated today with the concept of general benefits to the economy. The presence of mineral resources and centers of industry in close proximity to the waterway, in spite of its physical limitations, would allow the river to function as an important link within the transportation system, providing a cheap and efficient means of mass movement. Supplemental technological improvements on the Oder River tributaries and the linking of the Oder with the Vistula via a canal in the south would tend to extend the hinterland, giving favorable opportunities for the development of traffic. The present east-west connection between the Oder and the Vistula in the north via the Warta-Noteć Rivers and the Bydgoszcz Canal is inadequate in respect to the distribution of mineral resources and industry.

The future volume of traffic which the Oder will be expected to haul is in part a function of the size of the hinterland and its predominant economic activity. It is expected that the important position of the natural resources in the economy of województwa Katowice, Opole, and Wrocław will persist despite the planners attempt to decentralize Poland's heavy industry. Therefore, it is likely that the subsequent expansion of industry and the further economic development of the five województwa will rely more heavily upon a fuller utilization of the Oder River as an artery of transportation which is capable of mass movement.

The Oder waterway needs to be looked upon as a specialized carrier, well adapted to moving large volumes at relatively low costs. However, to reap the full benefits of the advantages would require not only full integration of the Oder River as a mode of transportation within the nation's transportation system but also would require a greater degree of specialization among other carriers.

The Oder River as an artery of transportation for some time to come will remain a valuable waterway of internal domestic importance and in this direction the investments should be made. Since the location and directional flow of the Oder River is so important, particular attention should be given to its full utilization. The comprehensive exploitation of the river's capacity will considerably release the mounting pressure on the Silesia-Szczecin railroad line.

Appendix

TABLE A1

INTRAREGIONAL AND INTERREGIONAL MOVEMENT ON THE ODER BY TYPE OF COMMODITY
(IN TONS)

YEAR: 1970   REGION: KATOWICE

Type of Commodity	Consigned			Received			Balance of Shipment
	Total	Shipment Within Region	Shipment Outside Region	Total	Shipment Within Region	Shipment Outside Region	
TOTAL	984,390	----	984,390	563,313	----	563,313	+421,077
Coal	967,137	----	967,137	----	----	----	+967,137
Metal & Metal Products	11,961	----	11,961	17,992	----	17,992	-6,031
Sand and Gravel	----	----	----	151,058	----	151,058	-151,058
Ore	----	----	----	147,954	----	147,954	-147,954
Fertilizer	----	----	----	237,394	----	237,394	-237,394
Agricultural Products	----	----	----	293	----	293	-293
Wood & Wood Products	----	----	----	----	----	----	----

Source: Głowny Urząd Statystyczny, Przewozy Ładunków Żeglugą Śródladową Pomiędzy Województwami i Wojewódzkie Bilanse Przewozów Ładunków 1966-1970 Nr. 92 (Warsaw: July, 1971), Table 9/40, pp. 59-60.

227

TABLE A2

INTRAREGIONAL AND INTERREGIONAL MOVEMENT ON THE ODER BY TYPE OF COMMODITY
(IN TONS)

YEAR: 1970   REGION: OPOLE

Type of Commodity	Consigned			Received			Balance of Shipment
	Total	Shipment Within Region	Shipment Outside Region	Total	Shipment Within Region	Shipment Outside Region	
TOTAL	409,633	12,510	630,013	186,811	17,356	169,455	+222,822
Coal	245,372	----	245,372	21,686	400	21,286	+223,686
Metal & Metal Products	7,280	----	7,280	----	----	----	+7,280
Sand and Gravel	146,142	16,552	129,590	22,347	16,552	5,795	+123,795
Ore	----	----	----	89,406	----	89,406	-89,406
Fertilizer	611	----	611	22,817	----	22,817	-22,206
Agricultural Products	5,208	----	5,208	17,817	----	17,817	-12,609
Wood & Wood Products	----	----	----	2,018	----	2,018	-2,018
Misc. Products	----	----	----	540	----	540	-540

Source: Główny Urząd Statystyczny, Przewozy Ładunków Żeglugą Śródlądową Pomiędzy Województwami i Wojewódzkie Bilanse Przewozów Ładunków 1966-1970 Nr. 92 (Warsaw: July, 1971), Table 15/46, pp. 63-64.

TABLE A3

INTRAREGIONAL AND INTERREGIONAL MOVEMENT ON THE ODER BY TYPE OF COMMODITY
(IN TONS)

YEAR: 1970   REGION: WROCŁAW

Type of Commodity	Consigned			Received			Balance of Shipment
	Total	Shipment Within Region	Shipment Outside Region	Total	Shipment Within Region	Shipment Outside Region	
TOTAL	782,671	464,477	318,194	733,938	464,477	269,461	+48,733
Coal	292,375	----	292,375	132,017	----	132,017	+160,549
Sand and Gravel	464,477	464,477	----	464,477	464,477	----	0
Ore	----	----	----	5,067	----	5,067	-5,067
Fertilizer	----	----	----	123,942	----	123,942	-123,942
Agricultural Products	8,136	----	8,136	3,197	----	3,197	-4,939
Wood & Wood Products	----	----	----	404	----	404	-404
Misc. Products	1,464	----	1,469	639	----	639	+825

Source: Główny Urząd Statystyczny, Przewozy Ładunków Żeglugą Śródlądową Pomiędzy Województwami i Wojewódzkie Bilansie Przewozów Ładunków 1966-1970 Nr. 92 (Warsaw: July, 1971), Table 5/36, pp. 55-56 and Table 20/51, p. 69.

229

TABLE A4

INTRAREGIONAL AND INTERREGIONAL MOVEMENT ON THE ODER BY TYPE OF COMMODITY
(IN TONS)

YEAR: 1970   REGION: ZIELONA GÓRA

Type of Commodity	Consigned			Received			Balance of Shipment
	Total	Shipment Within Region	Shipment Outside Region	Total	Shipment Within Region	Shipment Outside Region	
TOTAL	76,331	----	76,331	1,142	----	1,142	+75,189
Coal	----	----	----	5,431	----	5,431	-5,431
Sand and Gravel	28,661	----	28,661	----	----	----	+28,661
Ore	----	----	----	----	----	----	----
Fertilizer	----	----	----	77	----	77	-77
Agricultural Products	965	----	965	346	----	346	+619
Wood & Wood Products	4,945	----	4,945	----	----	----	+4,945
Misc. Products	500	----	500	465	----	465	+35

Source: Główny Urząd Statystyczny, Przewozy Ładunków Żeglugą Śródlądową Pomiędzy Województwami i Wojewódzkie Bilanse Przewozów Ładunków 1966-1970 Nr. 92 (Warsaw: July, 1971), Table 21/52, p. 70.

TABLE A5

INTRAREGIONAL AND INTERREGIONAL MOVEMENT ON THE ODER BY TYPE OF COMMODITY
(IN TONS)

YEAR: 1970   REGION: SZCZECIN

Type of Commodity	Consigned			Received			Balance of Shipment
	Total	Shipment Within Region	Shipment Outside Region	Total	Shipment Within Region	Shipment Outside Region	
TOTAL	1,072,761	953,564	119,197	1,580,945	953,564	627,381	-508,184
Coal	78,058	53,549	24,510	325,842	53,549	272,293	-247,783
Sand and Gravel	871,654	844,391	27,263	844,391	844,391	----	+27,263
Ore	1,053	1,053	----	131,608	1,053	130,555	-130,555
Fertilizer	731	----	731	210,802	----	210,802	-210,071
Agricultural Products	29,305	3,133	26,172	5,377	3,133	2,244	23,928
Wood & Wood Products	21,196	18,958	2,238	18,958	18,958	----	-2,238
Misc. Products	17,436	17,436	----	20,827	17,436	3,391	-3,391

Source: Główny Urząd Statystyczny, Przewozy Ładunków Żeglugą Śródlądową Pomiędzy Województwami i Wojewódzkie Bilanse Przewozów Ładunków 1966-1970 Nr. 92 (Warsaw: July, 1971), Table 18/49, pp. 66-67.

231

Bibliography

Books

The American Waterways Operators, Inc. *Big Load Afloat*. Washington, D.C.: 1966.
_____. *Waterway Economics*. January, 1970.

Andrjansk, Stanisław. *Służba Liniowa Na Śródlądowych Drogach Wodnych*. Warsaw: 1956.

Beck, L. *Geschichte Des Eisens*. IV. Hermann Fuchner, "Geschichte Des Schlesischen Berg-Und Hutten- wesens in Der Zeit Friedrichs Des Grossen, Friedrich Wilhelm II and Friedrich Wilhelm III," Zeitschrift Fur Deutsche, B.H.U.S., XLVIII, 1900.

Beschoren, K. *Schieben und Ziehen in Schleppdienst*. Vol. XIII. Werft Rederei und Hafen, 1931.

Christaller, Walter. *Central Places in Southern Ger- many*. Englewood Cliffs, New Jersey: Prentice- Hall, Inc., 1966.

Dawson, Albert J. *The Development of Economic Potential of Inland Waterways Transportation*. Pittsburgh: Dravo Corporation, 1956.

Engineer Research Office. *Navigable Waterways of Germany*. Vols. II, VI, VIII, and XXXVII. Strategic Intelligence Branch, Military Intelligence Division, August, 1944.

Giesecke, Gerhard. *Oderschiffahrts und Oder Wirtsdiaftsfrzgen*. Emsdetten: 1940.

Główny Urząd Planowania Prezestrzennego. *Atlas Ziem Odzyskanych*. Warsaw: 1947.

Główny Urząd Statystyczny. *Rocznik Statystyczny 1971* Warsaw: 1971.

_____. *Przewozy Ładunków Żegluga Sródlądowa Pomiędzy Województwami i Wojewódzkie Bilanse Przewozów Ładunków 1966-1970* Nr. 92 (Warsaw: July 1971).

_____. *Rocznik Statystyczny Przemysłu 1945-1966*. Warsaw: 1967.

_____. *Rosznik Statystyczny Przemysłu 1967*. Warsaw: 1968.

_____. *Rocznik Statystyczny Transportu 1945-1966*. Warsaw: 1967.

_____. *Statystyka Transportu Kolejowego 1967*. Nr. 25. Warsaw: 1968.

_____. *Statystyka Żeglugi Sródlądowej i Dróg Wodnych Sródlądowych 1968*. Nr. 48. Warsaw: 1969.

_____. *Statystyka Żeglugi Sródlądowej i Dróg Wodnych Sródlądowych 1967*. Nr. 28. 1968.

_____. *Transport Wodny Sródlądowy*. Nr. 18. Warsaw: 1967.

_____. *Żegluga Sródlądowa i Drogi Wodne Sródlądowe 1971*. Nr. 120. Warsaw: 1972.

Grabania, Marek. *Regiony Przemysłowe Województwa Katowickiego*. Katowice: Śląski Instytut Naukowy, 1963.

Grodek, Andrzej (ed.). *Monografia Odry*. Poznań: Instytut Zachodni, 1948.

Hay, William W. *An Introduction to Transportation Engineering*. New York, New York: John Wiley & Sons, Inc., 1961.

Hofman, Łucjan. *Ekonomika Branżowa Jako Nauka: Na Przykładzie Ekonomiki Transportu*. Sopot: Wyższa Szkoła Ekonomiczna, 1962.

Holmberg, Nils. *Oderhndeln*. Lund: 1941.

Interstate Commerce Commission. *Transport Statistics in the United States 1965*. Part I: "Railroads." Washington, D.C.: 1966.

James, Preston E., and Jones, Clarence F. (eds.). *American Geography: Inventory and Prospect*. Syracuse: Syracuse University Press, 1954.

Janiszewski. *Atlas Geograficzny Polski*. Warszawa: Wydawnictwo Naukowe, 1959.

Kansky, K. J. *Structure of Transportation Networks*. Chicago, Illinois: Department of Geography Research Paper No. 84, University of Chicago, 1963

Kondracki, Jerzy. *Geografia Fizyczna Polski*. Warsaw: Państwowe Wydawnitstwo Naukowe, 1967.

Langer, William (ed.). *Western Civilization: The Struggle for Empire to Europe in the Modern World*. New York: Harper & Row, Publishers, Inc., 1968.

Lijewski, Teofil. "Niektóre Problemy Badawcze W Geografii Transportu Kolejowego." *Zeszyty Naukowe Szkoły Głównej Planowani i Statystyki*. Nr. 63. 1967.

Locklin, D. Philip. *Economics of Transportation*. 5th ed. Homewood, Illinois: Richard D. Irwin, Inc., 1960.

Magiera, Władysław. *Ekonimika Transportu Wodnego (Żeglugi Śródlądowej)*. Wrocław: Wyższa Szkoła Ekonomiczna w Szczecinie Nakładem Państwowego Wydawnictaw Naukowego, 1951.

Misiuna, Władysław. *Rolnictwo na Ziemiach Zachodnich i Północnych*. Poznań: Wydawnictwo Poznańskie, 1956.

Mossman, Frank H., and Morton, Newton. *Logistics of Distribution Systems*. Boston: Allyn and Bacon, Inc., 1965.

Mrzygłód, Tadeusz. *Politika Rozmieszczenia Przemysłu w Polsce 1946-1980*. Warsaw: Ksiażka i Wiedze, 1962.

Państwowe Przetrzembiorstwo, Żegluga na Odrze. *Przepisy dla Dróg Wodnych*. Wrocław: 1969.

Pegrum, D. F. *Transportation: Economics and Public Policy*. Homewood, Illinois: Richard D. Irwin, Inc., 1963.

Peters, F. *Bestimmung Der Leistung von Schleppzugwn*. Vol. XVI. Werg Rederei und Hafen, 1925.

Pounds, Norman J. G. *The Upper Silesian Industrial Region*. Bloomington, Indiana: Indiana University Press, 1958.

Prezydjum Rady Narodowej. *Regulamin Nawigacyiny Na Drogach Wodnych Śródlądowych Rzeczypospolitej Polski*. Warsaw: 1950.

Skorowski, Stanisław. *Geografja Gospodarcza Polski*. Warsaw: Wydawnictwo Naukowe, 1939.

Smith, E. A. *The Zinc Industry*. London: Longmans & Company, 1918.

Starr, Millard O. *A Comparative Analysis of Resistance to Motion in Commercial Transportation.* Unpublished Master of Science thesis, Department of Mechanical Engineering, University of Illinois, 1945.

Thomas, William L., Jr. (ed.). *Man's Role in Changing the Face of the Earth.* Chicago: University of Chicago Press, 1956.

Tuszko, Aleksander (ed.). *Zarys Planu Perspektywicznego. Gospodarki Wodnej w Polsce.* No. 8371, P.A.N. Warsaw: 1968.

U. S. Department of Commerce, Bureau of the Census. *Statistical Abstract of United States 1969.* Washington, D. C.: U. S. Government Printing Office, 1969.

Wydawnictwo Komunikacji i Łacznosci. *Rozkład Jazdy Autobusów P.K.S.* Warsaw: 1969.

_____. *Rozkład Jazdy Pociagów P.K.P.* Warsaw: 1969.

Zachodnich, Towarzystwo Rozwoju Ziem. *Żegluga na Odrze.* Wrocław: May, 1969.

Zech, Hans F. *Die Deutsche Wirtschaft und Sudosteuropa.* Leipzig: 1931.

Periodicals

Allen, J. F., and Walker, W. P. "Resistance of Barges in Deep and Shallow Water," *Transactions of the Institution of Naval Architects* (1948).

Barcinski, Franciszek. "Bogactwa naturalne ziem odzyskanych i ich znaczenie gospodarcze dla Polski," *Przeglad Zachodni,* Vol. III (1947).

Biuletin Państwowego Instytutu Hydrologicznego Meteorologicznego Nr. 5 (126) (May, 1969).

Dawson, Albert J. "Design of Inland Waterway Barges," *Transactions, Society of Naval Architects and Marine Engineers,* Vol. LVIII (1950).

Deutsch, Karl. "On Communications Models in the Social Sciences," *Public Opinion Quarterly,* Vol. XVI (1952), pp. 356-380.

Dziewonski, Z. "Odra w Gospodarce Ziem Odzyskanych," *Życie Gospodarcze,* No. 16a (1947).

Kaufman, J. H. "Planning for Transport Investment in the Development of Iran," *The American Economic Review*, Vol. LII, No. 2 (1962), pp. 396-404.

Kempf, G. "Economical Speeds in Shallow Water," *Shipbuilding and Shipping Record*, Vol. V (June, 1924).

Kolipinski, Jan. "Rola Ziem Odzyskanych w Organizmie Gospodarczym Polski," *Przegląd Zachodni*, Vol. II (1946).

Lijewski, Teofil. "Rozwój Sieci Kolejowej Polski," *Dokum Geogr.* (1959).

Magiera, Władysław. "Nakłady Investycyine na Drogi Wodne," *Gospodarka Wodna*, Nr. 1 (January, 1970).

Milkowski, Marian. "Aktualna budowa zbiornika wodnego w Raciborzu i Kanału Żeglugowego," *Gospodarka Wodna*, Nr. 7 (July, 1968).

"Oberschlesien als Standort einer Eisenschaffenden Industrie," *Vierjahresplan*, Vol. V (1941).

Orsztynowicz, Jadwiga. "Udzial Wód Podziemnych w Bilansie Wodnym Dorzecza Odry w Latach 1951-1960," *Gospodarka Wodna*, No. 4 (1969).

Owen, W. "Transportation and Technology," *The American Economic Review*, Vol. LII, No. 2 (1962), pp. 405-414.

Popiołek, Kazimierz. "Koncetracja i Centralizacja Produkcji w Górniczo-Hutniczym Przemyśle Górnego Śląska w Połowie XIX Wieku," *Kwartalnik Historyczny*, P.A.N., Vol. LXIII, Nr. 405 (1956), pp. 265-267.

Puczynski, Kazimierz. "Kanal Odra-Dunaj," *Gospodarka Wodna*, Nr. 6 (June, 1968).

Ryszka, Franciszek. "Kapitał Monopolistyczny Na Górnym Śląsku i Formy Jego Polityki," *Przegląd Zachodni* (1952).

Szczepankiewicz, Stanislaw. "Neo-Pleistocene Changes in a Large River Valley with the Oder as Example," *Geografiia Polonica*, (1970), pp. 23-33.

U. S. Congress. House. *Lake Erie and Ohio River Canal*. 76th Congress, 1st Session, House Document No. 178. Washington, D. C.: Government Printing Office, 1939.

Vasilevskiy, L. I. "Basic Research Problems in the Geography of Transportation of Capitalist and Underdeveloped Countries," *Soviet Geography: Review and Translation*, Vol. IV (1963).

Wolfe, Roy I. "Contribution from Geography to Urban Transportation Research," *Highway Research Board*, Bulletin 326. Washington, D. C.: National Research Council, 1962.

GENERAL REFERENCES

Books

Appleton, James H. *A Morphological Approach to the Geography of Transport*. Yorkshire: University of Hull Publications, 1965.

Becht, J. Edwin. *A Geography of Transportation and Business Logistics*. Dubuque, Iowa: Wm. C. Brown Company Publishers, 1970.

Berezowski, Stanisław. *Geografia Transportu*. Warsaw: Wydawnictwo Naukowe, 1962.

_____. *Regionalna Geografia Ekonomiczna Polski*. Warsaw: Wydawnictwo Naukowe, 1962.

Bigham, Truman C., and Roberts, Merrill J. *Transportation Principles and Problems*. 2nd ed. New York: McGraw-Hill, 1952.

Bunge, William. *Theoretical Geography*. (Lund Studies in Geography.) 2nd ed. Lund: C. W. K. Gleerup Publishers, 1966.

Burka, J., and Dziewiecki, M. *Organizacja i Technika Transportu Śródlądowego*. Gdynia: Biblioteka Ekonomiczna Transportu, 1965.

Czekanska, Maria. *Z Biegiem Odry*. Poznań: Wydawnictwo Zachodnie, 1946.

Daggett, Stuart. *Principles of Inland Transportation*. 4th ed. New York: Harper & Brothers Publishers, 1955.

Fair, Marvin L., and Williams, Ernest W., Jr. *Economics of Transportation*. New York: Harper & Brothers, Publishers, 1959.

Greenhut, Melvin L. *Plant Location in Theory and in Practice: The Economics of Space*. Chapel Hill: The University of North Carolina Press, 1956.

Gronowski, F. *Odra Jako Wylotowa Arteria Transportowa Na Zachodnio-Europejskie Drogi Wodne*. Szczecin, 1961.

_____. *Transport Wodny Sródlądowy*. Szczecin: Politechnika Szczecinska, 1963.

Haggett, Peter, and Chorley, Richard J. *Network Analysis in Geography*. New York: St. Martin's Press, 1969.

Horning, Alfred. *Komunikacja Na Górnym Śląsku*. Katowice: Śląski Institut Naukowy w Katowicach Wydawnictwo "Śląskie," 1963.

Hutchison, Graham Seton. *Silesia Revisited*. Simpkin Marshall, Ltd., 1929.

Isard, Walter. *Location and Space-Economy*. New York: M.I.T. Press and John Wiley & Sons, Inc., 1959.

Lambor, Julian. *Locja Rzeczna*. Warsaw: Wydawnictwo Komunikacyjne, 1953.

Leszcyski, Stanisław (ed.). *Zarys Geografii Ekonomicznej Polski*. Warsaw: Wydawnictwo Naukowe, 1967.

Losch, August. *The Economics of Location*. New York: John Wiley & Sons, Inc., 1967.

Mikolajski, J. *Transport Wodny w Polsce i Jego Problematyka Geograficzna*. Zeszyty Naukowe Politechniki Szczecińskiej, September, 1959.

Miller, E. Willard. *A Geography of Manufacturing*. Englewood Cliffs, New Jersey: Prentice-Hall, Inc., 1962.

Muszynski, H. *Żegluga Sródlądowa w Obsłudze Szczecina i Swinoujscia w Latach 1961-1965*. Politechnika Szczecinska, 1967. (Unpublished.)

Naval Intelligence Division. *Germany: Ports and Communications*. Vol. IV. (B.R. 529C, Geographical Handbook Series.) 1945.

Norton, Hugh S. *Modern Transportation Economics*. Columbus, Ohio: Charles E. Merrill Books, Inc., 1965.

Petrazycka-Loth, J. Z. *Geografia Gospodarcza Polski*. Warsaw: Wydawnictwo Ekonomiczne, 1962.

Richlowski, Bogumil. *Województwo Katowickie Zarys Geograficzno-Ekonomiczny*. Warsaw: Wydawnictwo Naukowe, 1967.

Riedela. *Drogi Wodne w Planie 6 Letnim*. Warsaw: Wydawnictwo Techniczne, 1952.

Rudzki, Adam. *Polish Transport: Organization and Economics*. New York: Mid-European Studies Center, 1955.

Rutkiewicz, Ignacy. *Sprawy Welkiej Rzeki*. Wrocław: Zakład Narodowy im. Ossolinskich, 1961.

Ullman, Edward L. *American Commodity Flow*. Seattle: University of Washington Press, 1957.

Zauberman, A. *Industrial Progress in Poland, Czechoslovakia and East Germany 1937-1962*. London: Oxford University Press, 1964.

Periodicals

Beckmann, Martin. "Principles of Optimum Location for Transportation Networks." Symposium on Quantitative Problems in Geography, sponsored by the Office of Naval Research, Chicago, May 506, 1960.

Brown, S. Earl, and Trott, Charles E. "Grouping Tendencies in an Economic Regionalization of Poland," *Annals of the Association of American Geographers*, Vol. LVIII, No. 2 (June, 1968), pp. 327-342.

Garrison, William L. "Spatial Structure of the Economy: I," *Annals of the Association of American Geographers*, Vol. XLIX (March, 1959), pp. 232-239.

_____. "Spatial Structure of the Economy: II," *Annals of the Association of American Geographers*, Vol. XL (December, 1959), pp. 471-482.

240

_____. "Spatial Structure of the Economy: III," *Annals of the Association of American Geographers*, Vol. L (September, 1960), pp. 358-373.

Greenhut, Melvin L. "Integrating the Leading Theories of Plant Location," *Southern Economic Journal*, Vol. XVIII (1952), pp. 526-538.

Isard, Walter. "Interregional and Regional Input-Output Analysis: A Model of a Space Economy," *Review of Economics and Statistics*, Vol. XXXIII (1951), pp. 318-328.

Pounds, Norman J. G. "The Industrial Geography of Modern Poland," *Economic Geography*, Vol. XXXVI, No. 3 (July, 1960), pp. 231-253.

Taaffe, Robert N. "Transportation and Regional Specialization: The Example of Soviet Central Asia," *Annals of the Association of American Geographers*, Vol. LII (1962), pp. 80-98.

Ullman, Edward L. "Rivers as Regional Bonds: The Columbia-Snake Example," *Geographical Review*, Vol. XLI (1951), pp. 210-225.

Index

243

244

245

246